Explorations in
Consciousness

Explorations in Consciousness

Atala Dorothy Toy

THE CROSSING PRESS
FREEDOM, CALIFORNIA

For information on bulk purchases or group discounts for this and
other Crossing Press titles, please contact our Special Sales Manager at
800/777-1048.

Visit our Web site: **www.crossingpress.com**

Library of Congress Cataloging-in-Publication Data

Toy, Atala Dorothy.
   Explorations in consciousness / by Atala Dorothy Toy.
     p. cm.
   Includes bibliographical references and index.
   ISBN 1-58091-032-7 (pbk.)
    1. Consciousness--Miscellanea. I. Title.

BF1999 .T647 2001
291.4'36--dc21   00-064436

This book is dedicated with deepest gratitude to my spiritual teacher, Sri Chinmoy.

And also to my brother Chet Perry; my sons Steven and Brian Toy; my editor Caryle Hirshberg; and all the friends and family, guides, and students with whom I have had the privilege to walk parts of my beauty-road.

Table of Contents

Exercises

1
A Basic Understanding
of Consciousness

Success or failure, peace or anger, a good or bad job, a fulfilling or frustrating relationship—all of these embody a specific consciousness we're either trying to identify with or eliminate from our lives.

This workbook provides you with a practical understanding of consciousness: what it is, how it works, and how you can utilize it to achieve your personal and professional goals. You will explore the topic of consciousness from its highest unmanifest source through its descent into the forces and objects of our material world. Exercises are provided so that you work with the topics being discussed.

We will explore different concepts of the ultimate

source—where consciousness originates—and examine how consciousness takes form as thoughts, feelings, and physical existence. Knowledge of this process helps us understand how and why events and incidents happen to us in our lives. We will also show you different processes by which you can affect the consciousness that pervades your life.

There are people called yogis who have been studying consciousness for thousands of years. Their knowledge forms a body of inner sciences called, collectively, yoga. Like Western-based outer-world oriented sciences, this Eastern-based inner-world oriented science is empirical. It is based on knowledge that comes from direct, reproducible observations and experiences. Like the outer sciences, yoga has terms that are specific to its study.

Yoga is the science of union. It is a very useful method of understanding for this global era. It seeks to understand the common source of the universe and to experience it as well. Yoga is all-embracing. Whatever it encounters it recognizes as another method of understanding and working with the same one substance. It sees oneness everywhere and accepts multiplicity as the manifestation of the one source. This is the energetic orientation of this book.

Exercise 1:
Experiencing Consciousness

To experience both the oneness and the multiplicity of con-

sciousness, let's look at a universally appreciated type of consciousness, peace.

Take a clean piece of paper and write PEACE at the top. Then, write down words that describe peace to you.

Next, add words that describe other understandings of peace. For example, what peace means to an infant, a quiet child, boisterous child, teenager, ambitious career-oriented person, drunken street bum, mother, father, middle-aged person, elderly person. Write down words that describe what peace means to an athlete, scholar, scientist, politician, musician, mystic, farmer, city dweller, desert dweller, forest dweller, recluse, socializer. Write down words to describe what it means to different religious viewpoints: in relationship to the alleviation of social problems and injustices, to keeping commandments, to keeping the spirit of the law, to the mystical identification with the religion's founder or source. Look again inside yourself. What types of peace do different levels of your own existence want to experience: your soul, heart, mind, emotions, and physical body?

By now your list is quite long. What a rich, complex substance peace is!

Let's look at peace in a different way. Put down your pen and paper. For approximately two minutes close your eyes and feel the presence of peace inside yourself. Don't think peace, just be peace.

When you open your eyes, ask yourself: Which experience is truly peace? Is it the unified feeling you just entered into? Is it the multiplicity of forms and purposes you listed on the paper? Is it all these things put together? How is that possible?

As the quality of peace moves up the ladder of consciousness, it returns to its source, which is a state of unified oneness. As it moves down the ladder, it separates into a multiplicity of forms, each of which embodies some one aspect of the broad universal consciousness of peace.

There is a cooperative partnership between the universal inner quality of peace and its manifestation in material forms; that is, between consciousness and matter. These are magnetic polarities; each needs the other. The consciousness of peace needs a form for its manifestation. Form needs the quality of peace for its fulfillment. If a form does not permit peace to enter into its existence, and if the unmanifest consciousness of peace cannot find a form to flow into, both sides continue to exist but neither is fulfilled; each feels incomplete.

Waiver

If you want to solve all the problems of your life in one fell swoop, all you need to do is identify with the core source, or consciousness, of the universe. It's that simple. This one unified source has the capacity and is eager to be one with you and to be present in and with you at all times. When you establish this oneness, you need nothing else — no books, no teachers, no preset goals. All you need will be provided, in the absolutely correct time and form. You don't need this book.

Achieving this union with the source is the whole objective of the Earth game. This game works on multiple levels. It is difficult to play if we only see the details. It gets easier as we understand and master the principles, and practice. This goal is so challenging, says spiritual master Sri Chinmoy, that while there have been many individuals who have partially succeeded, very few in all of human history have fully achieved true mastery of this subject. However, this is no different from any other discipline. Not everyone can win the gold medal at the Olympics in the 100-meter sprint, but everyone can have the joy of sprinting to the best of their ability.

Until very recently, most people have had to focus on fulfilling the physical necessities of existence — protecting themselves and their loved ones from the elements, finding food to eat, fighting off predators. Through our concentrated efforts, we have, in general, created communities of different sizes to help us meet these needs. We are now working to stabilize this protection not only at a personal and community level but also at the global level. To succeed in mastering the many aspects of this very basic need, humanity as a collective conscious-ness has gradually become so focused on the physical details that it has lost its ability to work with the more subtle levels of existence. Today we are in the process of reawakening this innate human capacity.

If you, too, have been focused on these details and can't see the forest for the trees, this book will give you a broader perspective and tangible exercises as well. Once you learn to work with consciousness, how you choose to proceed to solve your own personal issues is up to you. No book or teacher can solve your issues for you. They are uniquely your own. They make up your own personal and ultimately fulfilling human game.

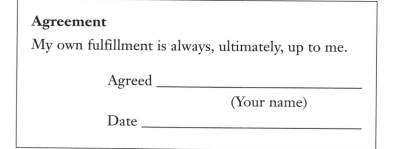

Agreement

My own fulfillment is always, ultimately, up to me.

Agreed _____

(Your name)

Date _____

Where We Are Now

The collective consciousness of Earth is beginning to work at a higher level of awareness to solve our common issues, which range from physical protection to spiritual fulfillment. This new level of awareness has come about through the process of evolution — a process that is such an inherent part of our planet's growth that visionaries of many cultures have been predicting this period for millennia. Terms used to describe it include the new age, the sixth world (Native American), the Aquarian age (astrology), the globalization of culture, the second coming of the Christ consciousness, the age of consciousness, and the golden age of spiritual awareness.

Some disciplines warn us we are approaching the end of the world. We are, but in a positive fashion. It is the end of the world we knew, with its sense of separativity, and the start of a new world of oneness-awareness. It is a world of heightened consciousness where the barriers between dimensions are softening. We are all having new experiences not fully explainable according to old paradigms. These direct experiences are forcing us to re-examine our perceptions. New rules and new parameters are needed. This need is resulting in the development of hundreds of subtle disciplines and modalities that enable us to see and work with the force/energy/light/consciousness that we now recognize creates the forms of our world.

Some of these new disciplines are based on the insights of ancient or contemporary visionaries; others on information channeled or transmitted from beings or forces who exist on subtle planes of consciousness. Knowledgeable human practitioners have become interested in how consciousness affects specific aspects of our health and have focused their efforts on scientific exploration and development. All this work benefits us greatly.

However, not only do roads lead to different realms of helpful consciousness, there are roads that travel into the dominions of the dark forces as well. These are sometimes disguised, or booby-trapped, as fun or scenic options. They can lead to problems.

Our new explorations are creating the need for consciousness maps so we can see where various roads are going, avoid traps, and travel safely to our chosen destination.

To solve any issue in our lives, we are recognizing that we must work at many different levels. No matter where an issue originates it eventually affects many different levels of our personal consciousness: physical, emotional, mental, and spiritual. To understand this, we can look at the relatively simple matter of a medical situation:

You have not been feeling well and you go to a doctor to find out what is wrong. The problem is diagnosed as a blood sugar imbalance, known in medical terms as hypoglycemia. What do you do now? How are you going to deal with this situation?

One approach is to deal with the issue as a physical body problem. A doctor trained in Western medicine, which traditionally favors this approach, might tell you that hypoglycemia is a chronic or hereditary ailment and recommends that you control the condition with medication, vitamins, and a change of diet. These types of basic physical approaches are most effective in crisis situations where one has to act fast to protect the physical body. So, in this case, when you take vitamins and change your diet, you feel better immediately; when you don't, you feel worse.

Eventually, however, you may tire of *controlling* the situation and feel you want to *change* the situation. This can take you into the realm of the healing disciplines, ancient and new, that work with subtle energy, a level of awareness that begins just above the physical energy level. These disciplines include herbal therapy, aromatherapy, Bach essences, Chinese medicine, Ayurveda, homeopathy, kinesiology, acupuncture, acupressure, and various counseling therapies. These disciplines are interested in how subtle energy blockages occur and how to alleviate the blocks so that energy can circulate properly. When energy is properly flowing, the body has the opportunity to heal itself. These disciplines might treat hypoglycemia as a subtle physical weakness in the adrenals, as an energy blockage or imbalance, or as a manifestation of a feeling such as being overwhelmed by the burdens of life. While the modalities practiced by these disciplines work more subtly and sometimes take a while to have an observable effect, the return to good health is often integral. "Integral" in yoga refers to the integration or interconnection of a body's multiple energy/consciousness systems.

The next option up in the field of consciousness is to go to a group of practitioners who deal directly with light and energy as healing mediums. We currently categorize these healers as lightworkers or energy workers because they are working with these consciousness substances. Lightworkers focus on fixing strands of light and removing subtle presences that are blocking an individual's energy. They want to get light flowing again through the part of the individual that has been affected. This type of healing is as ancient as human history itself and has been continuously practiced in many parts of the world, although it has been out of favor in Eurocentric culture for the past several hundred years. With the advent of our new era of awareness, an appreciation for these disciplines is resurfacing in the West. There are many different types of light or energy healing. Practitioners include psychic and spiritual healers, shamans and medicine people, advanced spiritual adepts (such as some yogis and some Buddhist monks), clairvoyants, channelers and unconscious healers (such as Edgar Cayce), psychic surgeons, time line specialists, and occultists.

These modalities might view the case of hypoglycemia as a symptom of a higher issue that needs to be solved before the physical manifestation (hypoglycemia) can be resolved. If, after treatment, the individual can retain the light, the problem is permanently gone. If darkness creeps back in from related issues that still need to be resolved, known as energetic "hooks," the problem may return or resurface in some other way.

The highest level of healing comes from the great spiritual masters of Earth's history. Included in this group are Christ, Buddha, Krishna, and also several living masters. Whether these great masters are living or dead does not matter, for they have transcended our normal perceptions of time and space. The healing of an illness such as hypoglycemia is not their primary concern. They are seeking to help humanity attain oneness with the source (God, the void, the Supreme). But because they are so compassionate, they will often intervene if a devotee prays for assistance.

These spiritual figures help by serving as messengers between the source of all existence and ourselves. If the source sanctions it, these masters can work at a very high place, from the soul to the physical body, to properly reconnect an individual with source, which then results in an immediate, permanent, and "miraculous" cure. True masters always state in simple open honesty that this cure is a gift of the source, not of themselves.

This ultimate level of human awareness comes with its

own set of parameters. If source tells the master that an individual's problem—in this case hypoglycemia—exists for the specific purpose of teaching the individual or someone else a necessary lesson that has not yet been learned, the master is powerless to intervene. However, masters are always permitted to pour light into the human consciousness; if the individual accepts this gift of light, they acquire the personal strength to solve the causative or karmic issue.

The different levels at which healing takes place also apply to all areas of Earth activity. We need to protect the physical structure of life on our planet, and for that reason the physical disciplines or institutions that have evolved are essential. These include the protection offered by governments, the military, and social services. Although we have succeeded in creating these institutional structures, they still are not completely fulfilling their visionary purpose—to assist society, not oppress it.

We are now discovering that a physical structure of any sort is simply the vehicle for holding thoughts and feelings and originating concepts. Therefore, we are now devoting time to learning how to move behind a physical form to positively shape its consciousness at higher, more malleable points. For instance, America has succeeded in legally abolishing slavery but now we must also change the attitudes on which it was based or its subtle energy will keep resurfacing in other areas on other issues. This issue has "hooks" that secure it on many levels of consciousness to individuals and to our society in much the same way as our example of hypoglycemia.

You can learn to see, feel, understand, and affect the process by which consciousness descends into form. Working initially in a controlled environment will help you focus on the separate elements necessary for success in the mastery of consciousness. It will help you immensely if you will set up for yourself a personal consciousness laboratory. All disciplines set up such sites, to explore and master issues pertaining to their study. This site is known by different names, according to its discipline: a gym, stadium, dance studio, library, clinic, office, meditation area, shrine or church.

A site that is created and maintained well functions well because the intense focus of its occupants is on a particular activity or issue and has been for a long time. The consciousness of their discipline has gradually and steadily enriched that specific physical site. The moment its users think of it or enter into it, they enter into its specific span of consciousness.

Shrines are prevalent in any society that wishes to hold, at a physical location, a subtle energy, consciousness, or spirit (Fig. 1). Shrines appear frequently in the Far East, in some Catholic and Christian communities, and among indigenous peoples throughout the world. In these cultures, shrines are often placed by individuals in some location they feel needs to be energized with good forces. This might be at an accident site, multiple locations around their home and yard, key locations in a community, at the cash register of a business, and even in the middle of a store's doorstep. A temple or church houses a communal shrine. A shrine is a powerful means of focusing light/consciousness so that it can work on Earth in a specific way for a specific function. You can look at it as a subtle-energy version of the laser machines we now use to focus light for a variety of technological functions such as cutting paper, reading bar codes, and operating on tumors.

Exercise 2:
Setting Up Your Shrine

If you have never created a personal shrine, this exercise will explain what it consists of and how to make one for yourself. Remember, though, this information is intended only as a starting point to help you create your own very individual shrine.

Select a location for this site in your living space that is quiet and has little traffic. If necessary, you can make a private, portable shrine in a box that can be closed up and put away when not in use.

Center a clean table in your shrine area, at eye level—

Fig. I
A sample shrine

high if you will be sitting on a chair in front of the shrine or low if you will be sitting cross-legged on the floor. Cover the shrine table with a clean, inspiring table covering—light pastels, pure white, natural fibers, cloths with silver or gold threads, or whatever your preference is.

On the table and within the shrine area you are going to place objects. These tools will help you concentrate your focus as you work with consciousness. Your shrine also serves as a place for composing yourself when you are under stress and a place where you can concentrate and identify with different aspects of consciousness to receive help. Each person's space will be different, for it will reflect their specific focus, culture, needs, and interests. Over time, your work will create a beneficial consciousness at your shrine that is uniquely your own. It will embody the specific energies you are calling on to help you work with your particular combination of issues.

Carefully select one item to serve as the center of focus on your shrine. It should be whatever you consider most important to your inner growth, although this may change later. You may wish to place a photograph, drawing, painting, or emblem of a specific individual who serves as a role model and in some cases as a protector and teacher for you.

If you are genuinely interested in learning about the workings of the universe, it is invaluable to have as a guide some very advanced teacher who has walked that path and actually reached the goal you are seeking. Advanced teachers have already blazed trails through many levels of reality; they know the pitfalls and can guide you through your own journey both inwardly and outwardly. Each teacher's way is slightly different, but each will take you to the same common destination because there is only one ultimate source of all creation.

On Earth, the very highest level of conscious human awareness has been achieved by the great spiritual figures of our history. If you have an affinity for Christ, Buddha, Krishna, Mother Mary, or some other high spiritual person, this is an excellent choice for your prime focal point. These greatest of all teachers are able to serve as guides for many people because they have transcended the limitations of the human body which is bound by time and space. They now exist as forms of universal consciousness, accessible to all who sincerely call upon them and identify with their consciousness.

Working under the protection of an advanced teacher gives you the confidence to be more daring in your explorations, for you very quickly learn that they are capable of assisting you no matter where your sincere efforts have taken you.

There are other options. Some people prefer a symbol of consciousness, such as a Star of David, a cross, or a mandala. As we will explain later, each of these symbols represents a different specific type of consciousness. When you focus on a symbol, it helps guide you into its domain. You can also choose a drawing, photo, or symbol of a saint, sage, god, goddess, or inner guide; or an inspiring quotation or passage from a holy book.

If none of the above-mentioned embodiments of consciousness appeal to you right now, you can receive help from nature itself and place on your shrine an object that inspires you and represents to you the consciousness you are seeking. This might be a photo or painting of a sunrise or sunset, an ocean, a waterfall, or a peaceful forest. Even a solitary seashell, stone, or pine cone can become a profound object of focus on your shrine, if it means something to you.

On my shrine, some objects stay and others come and go. Temporary objects are placed as a focus of immediate study and, once understood, they are reverentially removed, thanked with gratitude for their assistance, and returned to nature or placed somewhere else in my home. Similarly, you can place on your shrine various objects you wish to examine and understand, problems you seek solutions for, goals you seek to achieve. This is a way of offering up a challenging situation to God, the source, or the universe. These objects can remain on your shrine for a day, week, or month and removed whenever that issue is resolved.

Finally, you can incorporate objects into your shrine world that help set a relaxed, introspective mood such as flowers, incense, candles, crystals, and inspirational music.

You can make a portable shrine if your living circumstances require that you close it up after use or if you travel a lot. To make a portable shrine, find a box that is small but can hold all your shrine objects. Include in the box a small scarf which, when laid out, indicates you have temporarily designated this area for your work. On top of this scarf, place the central object of your focus and whatever other implements you wish to use.

Practicing At Your Shrine

Your shrine is where you will be exploring consciousness

in its most subtle aspects and developing the clear insight to apply this knowledge in your life.

As you start learning to examine and identify with consciousness, you can save time and improve results if you will practice regularly at your shrine. In this way you are steadily strengthening the positive consciousness of this area, which helps strengthen you.

Developing inner awareness is simply developing a more subtle human capacity than you are used to. You can see it as another type of muscle that with practice can become very strong and of weight-bearing assistance to your life. Just like working out at the gym, regular focused practice is a key element to the growth of inner awareness.

Set aside a minimum of five minutes every day for inner exercise at your shrine to strengthen your inner muscles. Make this part of your normal daily routine like brushing your teeth before you go to bed. Ideally, your consciousness muscle building should take place as soon as you get up in the morning. If you live with others, you might wish to get up five to ten minutes before them. Your session can be at other times as well, especially in the beginning. Evening is another auspicious time. Arrange to be undisturbed during this time; muffle your phone, inform your co-habitants, and find a way to occupy children.

It's important to clarify and state your intent when working with consciousness. In each exercise in this book, the intent is explained. Since this workbook emphasizes developing awareness, you will learn how to enter into the experience of the exercise and then, as a budding inner scientist, learn how to examine your experience. In Chapters 2–5 you will begin integrating the two polarities: the experience itself and the scientific observation of the experience.

Each person has an individual intuitive way to comprehend energy and consciousness. One person may prefer sound and so a soothing piece of classical music or a church hymn helps them to relax and center. Others may be more easily inspired by sight, smell, taste, thought, or touch. The exercises in this book cover a broad range of sensory capacities. You may find you have more initial success with some than with others due to your own personal orientation. However, please try them all because each provides a unique way to acquire knowledge about the workings of consciousness. You can repeat frequently the ones that especially appeal to you.

Exercise 3:
Your First Session at Your Shrine

There are two aspects to your work at your shrine. One aspect is your communication with the guiding consciousness you choose to work with; the other is the intent of a specific session such as acquiring peace, balance, or joy in some aspect of your life. Connecting with a guide is of primary importance because your guide clears the way and assists you in reaching your goal. This guide, as we have discussed, can be a being such as Christ or Buddha, or a concept such as peace. In this exercise you are going to begin connecting with a guide.

The first thing to do when sitting down at your shrine is to energetically open it for business. This includes lighting incense and candles, turning on music, and settling down in a comfortable and relaxed position. Place a clock or watch in the area and tell yourself that no matter what you experience, you are going to remain there for at least five minutes. Although this is a mere five minutes of exercise out of the 1,440 minutes that form your day, it can seem like hours if you have never before consciously sat still in silent reflection. Now rest your hands quietly in your lap, on your knees, or over your heart in prayer position. Then take some deep, slow breaths to calm yourself.

You will now begin to establish the overall guiding consciousness of your shrine. Start by offering the shrine area your gratitude, appreciating each part, and settling your attention on the central object. Offer this central object your gratitude, express to it that you are seeking the highest good, and ask for its help and protection as you undertake your work. Follow this procedure every time you sit down at your shrine.

This first time you sit at your shrine, ask yourself and the central object why you selected it to occupy the most important position. What was your unconscious or conscious intent? Sit silently, focusing on the object, and feel its presence permeating the shrine area, including yourself. When you receive an answer to your questions—the object may represent love, peace, wisdom, patience, God, mind, perfection, or some state of consciousness that you deeply appreciate—focus on seeing or feeling that quality very clearly inside the object. If you feel you have not yet found your true guide, ask the central object, the shrine, and all the positive forces of the universe to help you contact the real guide or consciousness you are seeking.

During this five minutes, stay seated even if no answer comes. You are building a bridge between yourself and the consciousness your shrine represents to you. Today you are throwing the first connecting cable.

If you wish, you can stay longer at your shrine, and you will be doing so as your inner muscles grow. But try to never spend less than five minutes. Even if you feel nothing is happening, it is. You are making movements in the world of energy and this world will eventually respond.

If you are inspired to do so, in addition to your morning meditation you can meditate for short periods of time throughout the day. Especially auspicious times to meditate

are noon, dusk, early evening when your chores are done,
and just before going to bed.

At the end of your five minutes, whether you feel you
succeeded or failed in this exercise, come back into the pres-
ent moment, offer gratitude to the world of consciousness
your shrine represents, and return to your everyday world.
This closes your session at your shrine.

The Inner Scientist

Each time someone searches for a particular type of con-
sciousness, such as peace, there is an empirically observable
progression. This is not something that happens all at once,
but can take place over days, weeks, months, and years.

First, work to define and recognize the consciousness you
are seeking so that you can invoke its presence. When you
feel the consciousness come to you, start working to solidly feel
this consciousness not only in the shrine area but also inside
yourself. Then establish a "warehouse" inside yourself where
you can store this consciousness for restocking during the day,
as needed. Eventually, you will create a steady flow from
your inner warehouse to your outer life. The next step is
bringing this consciousness into every plane of your existence
and every cell of your body, so that you and it are insepara-
ble. The final step is the ability and desire to offer this
consciousness to others. Depending on your orientation, this

can be the consciousness of peace or joy or it can be the energy of a specific cosmic master such as the Christ or Buddha.

There are many types of consciousness that each person embodies and offers to others and many guides in each person's life. But all of these guides are different from connecting with your own soul, which the Quakers call the "guiding light within." To truly live within the guidance of your own soul is the goal of all true spiritual disciplines.

Defining Our Terms:
Exactly What Is Consciousness?

According to Webster's *New World Dictionary*, "consciousness" is "the totality of one's thoughts, feelings, and impressions" and also "the state of being conscious." "Conscious" is defined as "aware" and "cognizant." The spiritual master Sri Chinmoy further defines consciousness in yogic terms as the substance of which all creation is made, yet existing beyond creation. It is infinite, eternal, immortal, and constantly transcending its own perfect perfection.

All definitions and descriptions of our universe and its workings are encompassed within consciousness as defined above. It is important to understand this for it is the basis of our work in this book. There is only one ultimate consciousness but it has many layers of manifestation. The following exercise will assist you in understanding this concept.

Exercise 4:
We Are the Experience of One Consciousness in Many Forms

In the following visualization exercise your intent is to experience the oneness of life of which you are an integral part.

Imagine you are in the far reaches of outer space. You are that space—no shape, no form, just expanse. Using your inner telescope, begin focusing more and more specifically. This darkness contains inside itself hundreds of sparkling objects. Some of these are grouped together, creating massive forms, including swirling galaxies. Inside one of these is our solar system. It is a separate entity, yet it is, at the same time, a part of each larger whole. Identify with this reality. Next focus inside this solar system to find our planet Earth—a very beautiful, peaceful form with white clouds moving freely across its blue-green surface, unhindered by boundaries of any sort. Feel you are this Earth, in all its oneness-beauty, separate yet still part of each larger whole. Then find your country and identify with it in a similar fashion, and next your city, your home, your shrine, yourself. You exist as a specific object yet you are also part of each larger whole. Pause here and feel the peaceful oneness of this descent of consciousness into your form.

Now it is time to start your journey back. Remember, this limitless, formless universe was within you when you focused your attention on it. Therefore, you are already part of it, as you expand. See your specific, individual self as expanding consciousness. Grow to also include your shrine, then your home, your city, your country, your world, your solar system, your galaxy. Pause here and feel this vast oneness. You are part of a cosmic whole, one that retains its cohesion no matter how large or small its current focus.

To finish this exercise, gently bring your awareness back to your own body, open your eyes, and sit quietly for a few moments. Close by offering your gratitude to the guiding consciousness of your shrine.

The Inner Scientist

What did you feel like when you brought vastness down into a specific form? What did you feel like when you expanded your individual form to universal proportions? The basic component of all this was consciousness, which changed into different outer forms but was inwardly inherently the same.

What would have happened if you had visualized yourself expanding from your individual form to the infinite rather than the infinite to the individual? Could you have found your path home? It is always harder to explore new territory if you have not first seen it from a high surveillance point. Consciousness faces this problem in any field. When you have seen only the solid, gross physical, you have difficulty seeing yourself as part of many larger forms as well. Therefore, yoga and other introspective disciplines teach you how to experience subtle consciousness and connect this with the physical world. You build a path to move back and forth between the two, and finally learn to exist comfortably in both awarenesses at the same time. You develop the capacity to see the forest and the trees at the same time.

The Hundredth Monkey Principle

The yogis understand humanity as the experience of consciousness in physical form. Our human goal is to be fully aware of our true substance—unlimited, pure consciousness—and to enable that substance to act while in physical form. We just experienced ourselves as part of many larger physical forms. The same is true with consciousness. Our single consciousness is also part of many larger units. Whatever you do affects them, and what they are and contain can affect you. Injure or improve any part of this chain and you injure or improve the existence of the whole. Being kind to a neighbor may seem specific to your life. It doesn't, on the surface, appear to exert a global influence. Likewise, a tribal war in Africa may not seem relevant to your life. A single act, good or bad, may seem to be confined to a single area. But it actually reverberates around the globe and throughout the chain of consciousness. Therefore, anything you do to improve your own consciousness ultimately affects the whole. You matter in the most integral sense of this term.

This reality has become known in the realm of consciousness study as the Hundredth Monkey Principle. This principle began as a postulation, based on scientific observation, that there are energetic fields that connect different types or levels of consciousness no matter where its participating members exist on Earth. It emerged in a thirty-year study of wild Japanese monkeys, the Macaca fuscata, on the island of Koshima, Japan. It was originally reported by Dr. Lyall Watson and later utilized in the ground-breaking consciousness work of Ken Keyes. The scientists doing the study would drop sweet potatoes in the sand for the monkeys to eat. The monkeys liked the sweet potatoes but not the sand that covered them. One day an eighteen-month-old female they called Imo solved this problem by washing the sweet potato. Over the next six years, the scientists watched as more and more monkeys began copying this behavior—first among the young monkeys and some mothers of the young monkeys and gradually among more and more of this study group.

Then, in 1958, the monkeys in this group reached a critical mass, which Dr. Watson arbitrarily assigned the number one hundred, and suddenly almost every monkey on the island began washing their sweet potatoes as well. When the scientists investigated the behavior of monkeys on other islands, they found this same behavior had suddenly appeared there as well. In Western science of that time, there was no known scientific way the monkeys could have communicated with each other. It was thought that there must, therefore, be some common morphogenetic field that stretches across the islands by which the monkeys communicated.[1]

Mystics of all traditions have always understood this principle. That is why, when they choose to live in a cave or forest or ashram and dedicate their lives to prayer and meditation, they know they are serving the world. For they are feeding the common human consciousness with their aspiration. Today many aspirants are living in society and attempting to do this same thing, in the midst of all the activities and distractions of modern life.

The more people who share the same hope, ideal, value—or negative consciousness as well—the stronger this consciousness becomes among any group connected

---

1. See information on this study in: Lyall Watson, *Lifetide: The Biology of the Unconscious*. Ken Keyes, Jr., *The Hundredth Monkey*. Drunvalo Melchizedek, *The Ancient Secret of the Flower of Life*, *Vol. I*, p. 106.

to this action, no matter where on Earth they are physically located. Therefore, if enough people are determined to change a way of acting, nothing can stop the collective strength of their shared will to make it so.

Clarifying Semantic Differences

As we move to a global community, with global action, we are finding it necessary to understand the commonalities behind semantic differences. When mathematicians see dos, duo, two, ii, and 2, they know it refers to the same concept. This is also true when examining the substance of which our universe is made. Different words are used by different cultures to describe the same thing.

If you look behind semantic differences, descriptions of what one experiences when entering the higher planes of consciousness are, like the concept of 2, remarkably similar no matter what the religion, philosophy, or culture. That is, when concepts are discussed at the highest perceptual levels, descriptions are remarkably similar. However, every time a choice is made as to what form a consciousness should take so that it can successfully act in a very specific way, it narrows down the options associated with that consciousness. For example, as we experienced in Exercise 1, the universal quality of peace is different for a child, athlete, specific country, and so on.

People who exist primarily in the gross physical con-

sciousness are focusing on mastering universal consciousness as it applies only to their specific task. They are at the
moment not interested in perceiving how their situation
interacts with larger issues; for instance, personal peace
with global peace. Therefore, if you speak about such a
higher-level issue with them, they will tell you it does not
matter or it does not exist.

People who exist in the gross physical are interested in
their particular tree and have no interest in seeing the
larger forest to which that tree belongs. Extending this
imagery, other people may be interested in themselves and
a few trees around them; or will further extend to see a
grove of trees. And, near the opposite end of this spectrum,
there are individuals, such as some philosophers, who are
interested in the esoteric only. They tend to see the need
of the whole forest but are not interested in the material
needs of a specific, individual tree. People in consciousness
studies are aware that both visions must be connected—
the forest and the trees—if action is to be fully successful.
We are working with these connectors in this book so that
no matter where you are focused right now you can learn
how to perceive and incorporate the awarenesses and
capacities of other viewpoints as well.

As we did in Exercise 4, when relating the cosmos to our
selves, let's begin our discussion by looking at the vastest
aspect of consciousness. This is the nature of creation

itself. We'll look at some of the predominant descriptions of creation, from those who have studied this subject in depth. This way you can understand how you view the issue, and relate your viewpoint to those of others.

The central point of all philosophies and religions is first to establish the origin of life, second to establish the purpose of life, and third to determine what is needed to successfully achieve this purpose. Everything else is an observation on one of these three topics.

There are three basic descriptions of the ultimate source, or origin, of existence. It is a void from which all has come; it is an unmanifest fullness in which all creation exists, in potential; it is an animate, conscious Supreme Being.

The Buddhists speak of the ultimate source as a nothingness that is void of all existence. Atheists who say they believe in the existence of nothingness at the source of the universe are saying that this void is the ultimate source. Hindus and yogis also speak of the ultimate source as a nothingness but their understanding of its nature is different, for this is the nothingness of ultimate fullness: it contains, in unmanifest form, all of existence. Many schools of yoga experience the source as a being—the Supreme Being itself. Christians, Jews, and Muslims speak of the absolute source of all existence as a Supreme Being, and they understand this Being is a force as well.

The greatest distinction, therefore, is whether the ultimate source is an empty void or an unmanifest fullness. Many proponents of these two views see this distinction as the obverse and reverse of the same coin. Whatever the semantic definition, they say, both views perceive all creation as arising from a single, unified, unmanifest source and eventually returning to this same one universal, unmanifest source. They say, let's agree to disagree on the composition of this final absolute source—whether it is, technically speaking, a void or an unmanifest fullness—for it does not affect the commonalities that exist between us from this point down.

No matter whether one believes a void or an unmanifest fullness is the composition of the ultimate source, all religions and philosophies have commonly experienced the highest levels of existence as capable of acting both as a force (such as energy, light, consciousness, unconditional love and/or peace) and as a being. Therefore, to establish a common working vocabulary for all groups, the spiritual master Sri Chinmoy has chosen to use the term "the Supreme," signifying the highest, or supreme, level of consciousness. He leaves it to each individual to define this word according to their specific needs, direct experience, and cultural framework.

Sri Chinmoy also often uses "consciousness" and "the Supreme" interchangeably, with the following subtle differentiation. "Consciousness" refers to the core universal substance/non-substance in its aspect as an all-pervasive energy, and "the Supreme" refers to the core universal substance/non-substance in its aspect of an aware and conscious being with whom we can communicate. It is the same one substance but with a different aspect emphasized.

As the focus of this book is on understanding the energetic nature of the universe, we will be primarily using the term consciousness. We will also be referring to it as the source, which enables each person to apply their own understanding of its nature. However, please keep in mind that we know this energy to be sentient and capable of communicating with us at any time. It does so by assuming whatever form is most comfortable to the belief system and level of awareness of the individual concerned, whether this is as a goddess, a bright light, a burning bush, a quality such as profound peace, or the figure of Krishna, Christ, or the Virgin Mary.

One World, One Consciousness
It was not so long ago that it was impossible to imagine a common global spirituality that embraced the understandings of all religions, philosophies, and lifestyles. A great modern breakthrough in directly experiencing this oneness took place in the mid-1800s in Dakshineswar, India, through the life of a great Hindu yogi named Sri

Ramakrishna. Sri Ramakrishna, a devotee of Kali, a mother aspect of the Supreme, wished to experience the presence of the Supreme in all aspects of life. He attained this goal, achieving the very rare and advanced state of oneness with the universe called, in yoga, God-realization or self-realization. Yogis understand these terms to mean the same thing, for at the core of our self, in our soul, we are made of the pure consciousness of the Supreme. At that time there was considerable conflict between different religions and even within Hinduism, many believing that theirs was the only true way to attain the ultimate goal and to know God. Sri Ramakrishna believed that all sincere paths lead to the same goal and set out to personally prove this for himself. He succeeded, experiencing the ultimate source not only through all the different major branches of Hinduism, but also through other religions as well, including Buddhism, Judaism, Christianity, and Islam.

Sri Ramakrishna's work embodied the awareness of a common spirituality that transcends the demarcations of individual religions. It was a radical innovation for its time and heralded an emerging global vision of our world. From this point forward, there has been a gradually growing movement that today has become such a massive collective force—the Hundredth Monkey Principle— that it is a prevailing awareness in enlightened society.

In 1893 a World Parliament of Religions was held in Chicago, Illinois. This was the first time a global gathering of this type was held and marked the official acceptance in the West of non-Judeo-Christian understandings. Swami Vivekananda, one of Sri Ramakrishna's chief disciples, attended this gathering and preached, to standing ovations, the yogic understanding of the basic unity of all religion. He founded the Vedanta Society, which anchored the teachings of Sri Ramakrishna in the West.

In the twentieth century a series of earth-shaking events has spurred the growth of a global spiritual perspective. Increasing numbers of migrations have resulted from such human horrors as war, drought, and famine. These disasters have merged many cultures together, which has made it necessary for diverse cultures to accept others' traditions and ways of perceiving reality. This positive result of negative events has benefited us all.

To understand how these horrors have contributed to the beneficial expansion of consciousness, consider the great and ancient Tibetan Buddhist tradition with its knowledge of the workings of the inner worlds. This knowledge was kept as closely guarded secrets for centuries. As with many teachings, it was necessary to protect this knowledge from falling into the hands of those who would abuse it or abuse its practitioners. After the invasion of their country by China, the monks were forced to flee to escape persecution and death. But they carried with them their knowledge and made it openly available to the cultures in which they have taken refuge, which has benefited the entire world. Their leader-in-exile, the Dalai Lama, has become renowned for his compassionate work on behalf of global peace.

Other turbulent routes have also helped bring us to our current global vision. In the early 1960s the emerging new age culture in the U.S. began actively exploring any world tradition that had secreted away knowledge about the hidden nature of the universe—of consciousness—and seekers were openly defying the restrictions of that era's strict and often vehement ecclesiastical dogma. During this time, faced with mounting discontent at all levels of its own membership, the Roman Catholic Church convened a three-year Vatican Council to deal with issues of church doctrine and reform. During the first year, in heated discussions, the church decided to officially redefine "true religion" to include Protestant Christian faiths; the second year it extended the definition to include Judaism; and the third year, at the insistence of its own Far Eastern bishops, it extended the definition to include any valid non-Christian faith such as those of the Far East. Together with many other factors, this granted an official seal of approval by a very powerful Western force to openly explore and discuss different perceptions of the ultimate reality.

Additional factors during this period included the civil rights movement, which brought the Islamic faith strongly to America through the black community. The women's equal rights movement has brought a re-emergence of long-persecuted and repressed feminine spiritual knowledge.

From this point on, the expanding search for information on how paranormal experiences occur, and from where, has brought forward esoteric and mystical knowledges that had been long hidden by their adepts to protect them against misuse, charges of heresy, and life-threatening persecutions. These knowledges include Kabalistic Judaism, Christian mysticism, and Islamic Sufism. As these forms of knowledge have become more available, people are no longer regarding their own paranormal experiences as freak occurrences, or something sinful or crazy to be hidden away, but as valid forms of communication with other dimensions of consciousness. This has led to the retrieval of ancient traditions such as Celtic, Egyptian, Mayan, Atlantean, and Lemurian. Information is coming from such sources as archeology, past-life recall, and the universe's consciousness libraries. We are receiving channeled information, and conscious transmissions or communication of information from other dimensions of existence such as angels, inner guides, cosmic forces, collective entities, extra-terrestrials, meta-terrestrials, and time-travelers from our own future.

We are still in the process of learning to work with these subtle existences accurately, because while some information is authentic, other information comes from mischievous or hostile entities. In sorting through this plethora of information, a knowledge of the workings and principles of consciousness is more important than ever before.

To close this introductory chapter, let's go back to the earlier exercise on peace. Peace is going to be a very valuable implement in your own inner exploration toolbox. Peace calms down all the forces you encounter and provides you with clarity of the senses. This clarity enables you to proceed on your journey. It is like standing on a tall cliff and surveying the desert below. You can see the marker points that you need to keep in sight as you travel through your own internal wilderness. Throughout this book, we will practice many ways to experience peace. The following exercise is drawn from the science of pranayama—breath control—which yogis find very helpful for connecting with subtle life energy.

Exercise 5:
Experiencing Peace in Your Life Through
Breath Control

Sit down at your shrine and open it up. Now focus on your breath as it goes in and out. Let it become regular and quiet. Begin breathing in through your nose and out through your open mouth. See yourself breathing in peace, and breathing out worries, anxieties, and tensions. Do this for about a minute. Now that you are in a deeper relaxed state, close your mouth and breathe in and out of your nose, still concentrating on breathing in peace and breathing out tensions, for about another minute. Next, focus on making your breath so slow, gentle, and regular that if you placed a feather directly under your nose it would not flutter. To achieve this state, you have had to bring peace into your whole body. Now sit quietly and feel this peace. This peace is universal; it permeates the atmosphere at all times and is simply waiting for you to identify with its consciousness. Feel this peace flowing through the air and through every particle of every object: yourself, your shrine, your living space. Become peace for as long as you can. When you have finished, come gently back to awareness of yourself in your body. End by closing your shrine area.

The Inner Scientist

Was this a peace owned by a Jewish, Christian, Hindu,

Buddhist, Muslim, or atheistic group? No, it was simply the universal consciousness of peace, manifesting itself on earth through a specific form—you.

Where exactly does this inner peace, common to all faiths, countries, and people, come from inside this vast universe; this peace that will provide you with the clear sight necessary for your own internal self-knowledge? It comes from one source and exists inside seven different, specific planes of consciousness. You will learn about these seven planes in Chapter 2.

2

Seeing and Feeling Consciousness

Everything that exists is formed of consciousness—people, animals, plants, places, and objects. We, as one manifestation of consciousness, can communicate with other manifestations of this same common substance. It's just a matter of learning how.

On the physical plane, if you, as an English-speaking person, want to converse with a Spanish-speaking person, you must first learn the other's language; if you then want to speak with a German, you must learn that language as well. Even if you speak the same language you can still have problems communicating: "That's bad" means something negative to a grandmother and the opposite to her teenage grandson.

Language exists at the gross physical level of consciousness. You can also communicate at higher levels of awareness without the confinements necessitated by spoken words. The spoken word offers precision at one level. But it can obscure the actual thoughts and feelings of the message and it can also prevent different types of consciousness that are related at higher levels from communicating with each other. Cross-species communication—humans with animals, plants, minerals, cosmic forces, and inter-dimensional beings—takes place at these higher subtle levels of consciousness. Some cultures on Earth are comfortable with this type of communication but our Eurocentric society has become so focused on mastering the physical plane that we have forgotten we ever knew how to communicate in these ways. When it does occur, we are culturally required to pretend it did not, or that it was our imagination, or that the person is crazy. One of the only formats in which it is all right to imagine such communication is science fiction. In these "imaginings" humans often communicate with "alien" species through the means of a "universal communication device."

We need to expand the bands of consciousness on which we can communicate because many beings exist in other consciousness dimensions, or planes. For example, back in the 1970s when John Glenn landed on the moon, Sri Chinmoy and a group of his Western students were watching the event on television. The students saw only a single man on barren terrain but Sri Chinmoy, with his extended vision, saw many small moon beings, existing in a different dimension of consciousness, joyfully greeting their visitor.

We have the innate capacity to communicate subtly, but because of the social pressures exerted by our society we learn at an early age to either close down most of these abilities and discount them as imagination, or keep quiet about our abilities. Some of these capacities are acceptable, such as communicating with a beloved pet, as long as we apologize and say "It's almost like he's talking to me, but of course its just my imagination." Others can be included in the domain of self-improvement: we are permitted to use "mind over matter" to see ourselves as strong, conquer a weakness, or to project strength and confidence in a dangerous part of town, at a job interview, or in an important meeting. We are also permitted to "will" something to occur, such as we find in the many books written by people (like Norman Cousins) who have willed their recovery from a serious illness. These are examples of working with consciousness to affect the gross physical plane. Here "gross physical" refers to the solid material level of physical existence, the body.

Communication through consciousness can be accomplished through the expression of thoughts, feelings, images, and inner conversations without spoken language.

For example, people around the globe communicate with angels and have never said they couldn't understand the Archangel Michael because he was speaking in Arabic and they only spoke English or Russian! Christians throughout the world are in touch with Christ, even though his spoken language while on Earth was an ancient form of Hebrew, not African Shona, Finnish, or Spanish. Lightworkers, healers, and shamans throughout time have received much of their healing knowledge and capacity directly from plants and rocks, none of which have spoken languages.

Altering Consciousness

As soon as we begin consciously working with the many different forces that are behind physical form, our ability to change and manipulate matter and events becomes much stronger, both for good and for bad. So the quality and orientation of our consciousness becomes more significant the more aware we become. In our world's recent past, those who had methods to work positively with consciousness knew this well; they kept their knowledge secret so it would not be abused by those motivated by power, profit, anger, jealousy, and other dark forces. As knowledge of these planes becomes more readily available, it is very important for the sake of both ourselves and our world that we develop them in the right direction, moving toward light and not toward darkness.

Tales abound, in fiction and history, of battles between the forces of light and dark. These range from the downfall of Atlantis through misuse of subtle energy technologies (a situation many fear we are in danger of duplication today) to the battles in the movie series *Star Wars*. The potential power of subtle energy, for both creation and destruction, is so real that during the Cold War period both Russia and the U.S. began employing the services of psychics to study the potential uses of occult warfare, including remote viewing, psychically affecting morale, teleporting through space, and making troop movements invisible.

The level of our consciousness is a critical factor as soon as we move into the subtle realms of energy. It is for this reason that psychic and spiritual healers throughout the ages prepare carefully each time they use these energies. They humbly request assistance and protection from their personal guides and guardians, from the light-guides and guardians of their patients, and from any beneficial forces or beings who have an interest in the work at hand. When healers finish their work, they thank all of these same beings.

This invocation of assistance and protection is the original function of the offerings and prayers that are made on the altars of churches, mosques, synagogues, and temples throughout the world. It is why we recommend you call upon a guide in your own work. These invocations require conscious communication, focused between the individual and the energies or beings involved in a spirit of mutual love, respect, service, and especially in the spirit of gratitude. A conscious individual is very aware of the wide variety of good, bad, and mischievous forces that exist and of the extraordinary protection that a guide provides them for their work.

The Freedom of All Created Things

Our consciousness influences not only our own development but also the development of everything we own, build, and produce. We are creators in our own little universes. We need to be careful in what we create, whether it is music that can influence young people to be either violent or peaceful, or atomic power that can be used for bombs or medicine. Once we have released a new "object" (creation) into the universe, it begins its own life as a free and independent embodiment of consciousness with its own range of freedom. Everything has a certain range of freedom, like a dog on a leash, to decide where to go and what to do.

Exercise 6:
Communication on Different Planes of Consciousness

This exercise will increase your awareness of your ability to communicate on subtle planes of consciousness.

Begin by invoking the protective and enlightening presence of the central, beneficent consciousness on your shrine. Thank it for its presence.

Enter into a peaceful, meditative state. If you need help achieving this, practice the pranayama you learned in Exercise 5.

Once you are relaxed, look back in your life to some pleasant time when you communicated non-verbally with another life form, such as a person, pet, tree, plant, or rock. Although we may later repress the memory, most of us have experienced such communication at various times when we are peaceful and relaxed, when we feel deep love, or when we are called upon for assistance in an emergency. You may want to reach back into your childhood, which is usually a time of innocent and open communication.

Learning this type of communication includes acceptance not only of our conscious actions but of our unconscious ones as well. Let's go through the stages of acceptance right now.

When you have selected the experience you wish to focus on, acknowledge that it is real. Next, identify with the consciousness you were in at the time of this event. Enter into the experience itself: appreciate it, relive it, become it. When you are finished, return to your normal state of awareness.

The Inner Scientist

Now let's practice this sequence again. This time you are going to examine the experience for the purpose of understanding and replicating it—one of the objectives of both outer and inner scientists. You want to understand how you entered this state, so that you can do so again and again, in other circumstances, consciously at will.

So, how did this communication occur? Something moved you away from the bounds of normal perception and into a different space. You temporarily expanded your normal working band of consciousness. Look inside and examine what took you to this place, study its path. Then, while still in meditation, practice moving back and forth between this inner state of communication and your outer, ordinary awareness. You are practicing, on a more grounded level, the same process as Exercise 4, where you traveled from universal awareness to your specific self.

When you are finished, give yourself permission to remember this experience and slowly come back to the outer world. This is called grounding yourself. It is an important step in exploring the different levels of consciousness. One major problem people have when first approaching this study is learning how to connect their awareness of the inner worlds with their everyday lives. In times past, seekers would go into caves and forests to remove themselves from sensory interference as they explored the subtle realms. But this had its problems too, because people often lost the ability or interest to act in the physical world, which is much more limiting than the inner worlds. Today there is a tremendous effort to connect the two major realms, spirit and matter, so that the awareness and capacities of each is available to the other. Eventually, your capacity will develop to the point where you can pause, examine, and work at many of the stages through which consciousness turns into solid form.

Group Consciousness

Every human being is born as part of different groups who are bound by their need to resolve specific issues. The needs of the group are mirrors of each individual's personal issues. An individual may move on to identify with another group when these issues are resolved, are no longer relevant, or are too painful. The actions, thoughts, and beliefs of a group about a specific issue feed the collective consciousness, and it is subconsciously and/or consciously tapped into by others working on that issue, no matter where they are physically located (the Hundredth Monkey Principle).

Earlier in our history, communities were small and scattered and had little contact with each other. In this isolation, many different ways developed to cope with the core issues of human survival and fulfillment. These survival methods gradually evolved into different cultural experiences such as the European, East Indian, Native American, African, and Arab cultures. Each culture developed different ways to be the embodiment of consciousness in the human form. As we move to a global society, we have the opportunity to learn from each other's experiences as well as a responsibility to respect each other's accomplishments. Organizations like the United Nations and the Olympic Games are helping to facilitate this process in a peaceful manner.

In our global society, it is more important than ever to allow for differences, to respect and learn from each other, and, when we disagree, not to denigrate what another culture has learned, values deeply, and wishes to share with us. For example, some cultures value their ability to communicate directly with animals, gods and goddesses, and cosmic forces; they can do this very well and can show us how. Eurocentric society is a more physically oriented culture and our contributions are oriented toward developing technologies to harness natural forces; for example, telephones, televisions, the Internet, and lasers.

Sri Chinmoy, whose work is dedicated to the cause of inner and outer world peace, refers to all the different cultures of our world as petals on the same one flower. Each petal is separate, each has its own direct connection with the source, and each adds to the rich beauty of the whole. Let's experience this reality for ourselves.

Exercise 7:
One Source, Many Parts

In this exercise, your intent is learn to value the many ways in which you experience reality both as a whole and as a collection of separate but equally valuable parts. We are going to start at the smallest unit, yourself.

Place a daisy, a rose, or a lotus on your shrine. The shape of these flowers is considered by many metaphysicians to be representative of the nature of reality.

Enter into a state of relaxation and then focus your attention on the flower. Appreciate and admire its existence, which seeks only to add to the fragrance and beauty of its environment. Look at the blossom. Then look at how its overall unity is really the result of many individual and slightly different petals, co-existing peacefully. Look at how all the petals connect to the same core source, the heart of the flower. Sit for a few moments and enjoy this experience.

Now let's experience the reality of this flower inside yourself. Visualize placing the flower in the middle of your chest, which is the location of your spiritual heart, and feel it growing larger and larger until you are that flower. Feel that the heart of the flower is your own heart/soul and the petals surrounding the heart of the flower are all the parts of your own existence. Admire them, appreciate them, value them. What would you be without your eyes or ears or bones or emotions? Which part would you want to rip out and get rid of? None. All are equally important to the whole. Appreciate yourself and all the wonderful parts that make up you. Remain in peaceful appreciation for several minutes.

When you are ready, see the flower grow smaller and finally return it to your shrine.

The Inner Scientist

Now let's look at the significance of this experience. The flower could represent your life and all the issues that concern you. Which petals are shriveled or are too large or are missing? What issues do these represent to you? How can you correct your own life-flower so that all the petals are equally healthy?

You can also place the image of the flower inside the heart of any other group you want to experience or examine, whether it is your family, your business, your country, your world. Focus on the same one source common to that group. Then study the pattern of its petal-parts. Where is it off balance or out of shape? How can this be corrected? What can you do to assist this process?

This is one way that practitioners of sacred geometry study reality. Sacred geometry believes that consciousness can be seen as moving energy patterns.

Looking at Consciousness:
Three Different Perspectives

There are three major ways to view and study consciousness. These include the study of the forms of consciousness, the study of how consciousness descends from the source into matter, and the study of how matter ascends into spirit.

First Perspective:
Sacred Geometry

Sacred geometry studies the patterns consciousness moves through as it becomes form. Those skilled in this science can see and describe these patterns. Although there are some cultural differences in these descriptions, the core observations are the same.

As we have already discussed, the sacred scientists of the major religious and philosophical groups believe creation came from one original source. How each group understands the "how and why" of this original source determines how the entire culture approaches life. This original perception influences their understanding of all existence.

Here I would like to share with you the first basic steps through which the sacred scientist moves, because these are the ones most important to our study. From here, if this approach resonates with you, you can explore the dozens of schools offering in-depth information and details.

Zero, 0 or ◯ is a line that comes around on itself without beginning or end. ◯ represents the void, or ultimate unmanifest source, from which all comes forth and which is infinitely expandable and contractible. The presence of a zero in a society's base mathematical system indicates they are aware of the concept of nothingness at the source of all existence.

One. This is the starting point for some numerical systems and the next point for the others. One, ⊙, or ● represents the void, or common source, becoming aware of its own existence.

Two. ●● represents the source as it observes itself. It is both the observer and the object observed. It now witnesses its own existence.

Three. ⢁ ⢁ represents 1 (the observer or source) exploring 2 (the object being observed). One way an object is examined and defined is by determining what it is and what it is not. This polarity is represented by the two parallel dots, or poles, beneath or above the 1. When connected, forming a triangle— △ or ▽ —it indicates that the consciousness being observed occupies that entire space. Thus an observer can now examine any set of polarities, such as hot/cold, light/dark, peace/war, and all the variations that occur between these extremes and their common source.

In sacred geometry, a triangle is a very active shape, for it encompasses the process by which spirit becomes a manifest form. Triangles can emerge from any point in consciousness, in any direction, but the energetic principle remains the same. You can examine a triangle by itself, or in relationship to other triangles.

In the Far Eastern traditions, the downward projecting triangle signifies the consciousness of the male energy, the creator force, the vision consciousness, and the descent of consciousness to become creation. Its shape is seen to be that of the male reproductive organs. The upward projecting triangle signifies the consciousness of the female energy, the creation force, the manifestation consciousness, and the aspiration of creation to move upward to reach the source. Its shape is seen to be that of the feminine reproductive organs. Together, these triangles become a double-sided form. This shows the two poles held in balance by each other and the range of consciousness each has that will affect the other side. The central point shows a total balance of the two forces, which permits the common source to be felt/seen/known.

Male

Female

In Hinduism and Buddhism, the presence of a symbol in the center indicates what consciousness is being explored. Nothing indicates the void, a dot indicates the source is seen as a single point of unmanifest fullness, and the figure on the left indicates this schematic is examining the heart chakra.

Many of the world's great mandalas, or energy schematics, show some relationship that develops between emerging, existing, and overlapping triangles. A classic Western symbol showing this relationship is the Jewish Star of David.

The great classic mandala of Hinduism and Buddhism, the Sri Yantra Mandala (Fig. 2), examines the process by which the source manifests itself. The Sri Yantra Mandala starts with an upward facing triangle (indicating that this is an examination of the forces emerging from the feminine

Fig. 2
Sri Yantra Mandala

aspect of the unmanifest source, or the creation), and then triangles emerge from it in a growing complexity of interactions. Notice that although the mandala starts by examining the upward facing triangle, its evolvement very soon manifests downward facing triangles, once again balancing out the universal energies inherently present in any aspect of source. In some variations of this mandala, each sub-triangle is shown to embody a specific combination of consciousness that has its own color, sound, and presiding deity.

If one accepts this energetic understanding of the nature of polarities, it becomes the best statement possible for the necessity to value and hold in equal regard the feminine and masculine energies. To maintain balance and integral strength, both sides of this polarity must stay in balance with the other; if one side is strengthened at the expense of the other, it automatically creates instability in the entire construct. When male and female forces are balanced in any situation, whether it is in a home or a culture, it provides a very strong, balanced base for effective action.

This double-triangle shape is the molecular structure of quartz crystal (sometimes its points are shown connected into a tetrahedron). Quartz is thus resonating with the basic formative energies of the universe. This is an underlying reason why metaphysicians, priests, and shamans throughout history have been drawn to working with quartz, considering it a major sacred, balancing and healing tool.

Four, ⁛, ⁛, ⁛ is the Earth number. It represents the forces of the universe being held in place in physical form on Earth. It is considered a very static type of energy. A four shape is in its positive aspect a way to hold energy still and in its negative aspect a trap that keeps energy from flowing on.

When working with this energy, and to avoid being trapped within it, the Hindu and Buddhist practices provide its mandala users with energetic doors, for entering or exiting, on each directional side of the square. The recognition that one can become trapped in an energy field is understood by all experienced energy workers. Other cultures provide their workers with similar escape routes in their consciousness tools. These include the tassel that is present on malas, prayer beads and on Native American rugs, the crucifix on the rosary, the line from the center of a traditional medicinal sand painting to its edge, and the drumming in shamanistic travel. In its early years of development, Western psychology failed to allow for this, which may help explain why it had the reputation for endless therapy and regurgitating of issues.

Cultural Interpretations of Sacred Geometry
Throughout history, different groups have visually graphed

consciousness to represent themselves and their work. We call these forms symbols, yantras, mandalas, shields and, in today's commercial world, logos.

There are many different traditional yantras and mandalas in all societies, each graphing a specific aspect of consciousness. In the Far East, these diagrams contain very specific details, each part giving information to other initiates on exactly how to proceed in understanding and working with that particular aspect of consciousness. To understand the value of these energy schematics, let's construct one of the most basic mandalas, the Hindu symbol for creation emerging from the unmanifest fullness-source.

We start with a single dot, signifying the source is unmanifest fullness ●.

The next shape to form around this is the double-ended triangle, which indicates that to sustain creation the male (visionary) and female (manifestation) energies of the universe must both be present and in balance.

This shape is contained inside a circle ⊙ , indicating the infinitely expandable and contractible nature of the double triangle, which emerges from the source (the dot or the one) and is housed inside the source (the zero).

Next comes two layers of lotus petals, each inside a circle. The lotus petals are understood in Far Eastern traditions to represent the flowering of an energy; the number of petals indicates the vibratory rate  of the energy. Eight-fold flowering represents many things, including the eight-fold path and the four primary and four secondary directions of energy. A double circle of petals indicates the flowering of creation reverberates out profusely.

Next we have the square with its four doors, indicating the spiritual scientist is holding this shape still for examination, and is free to exit/enter at will.

The final shape looks like this:

Fig. 3
The Creation of the Universe

Other cultures have other profound methods to work with consciousness. The Chinese yin/yang symbol shows how the universe is kept in motion by the nature of polarities. When one side of a pair begins to dominate, it automatically manifests the seed of its opposite pole, which then begins to grow in strength until it manifests the seed of the opposite, and so on.

Native Americans have contributed the medicine wheel, the form they use to walk the circle of energies that compose any issue. With the help of this form, which is usually divided into four or more sections, the practitioner strives to bring each segment of the circle into balanced harmony with the others so that none dominate or control. In the beauty of perfect balance, the originating central energy of the issue has the opportunity to move freely.

Christians focus on the power of the cross, taking as the center of this energy the sacred heart of the Savior. They invoke the directional parameters of this consciousness when they "cross" themselves in the name of the Father, Son, and Holy Ghost. Some Western churches are now building large labyrinths, with a central cross, so that people can physically walk these healing, balancing patterns of life.

Jungian psychology and new age psychology use mandalas to help people resolve issues, sometimes asking patients to draw their own mandalas to help them clarify the energy patterns of their problems.

Today, computers are being used to graph the movement of consciousness. One example is the Mandelbrot set. In this, one basic formula, when graphed out repeatedly, becomes a field of complexly beautiful intersecting forms that often looks like a piece of Indian paisley fabric. You can see clearly here how one simple form can evolve into an infinite variety of shapes. However, no matter how complex it becomes, you will discover that any part of it, when closely examined, is actually formed of the same core energetic force (formula).

All of the sacred geometry approaches we have discussed work with the premise that there is one common core source of existence, which can be perceived if one can understand the energies involved. All of these systems perceive that the way to experience what is behind the form is to bring the forces into balance so that the source can first be seen and then attained. This is the principle behind the quality of detachment so honored in most energy disciplines. This is the value of truly discerning the polarities of any issue, and of working to bring them into balance with each other so that their true source can be seen.

Exercise 8:
Walking the Circle

An understanding of sacred geometry can help you resolve personal conflicts. Let's examine the elegantly simple and profound Native American medicine wheel. Traditionally, Native Americans believe in "walking the circle" before coming to a major decision because they believe that consciousness must be fully balanced for optimum clarity. All points on the circle must be heard from with respect. Native American visionaries have assigned directions and qualities to each of the four major points and directions. Top = north, winter, inner wisdom. Right = east, spring, new growth. Bottom = south, summer, fullness. Left = west, fall, the harvest. The center point represents the Great Spirit, the core, and the central issue of the moment.[1]

Select an issue or conflict you are experiencing in your life. Draw a circle and place a dot in the middle to represent that issue. Then place dots at the top, bottom, right, and left and draw a cross connecting them. Mentally assign them the qualities described above. Choose a direction to enter and begin there to map out the movements of your issue—the north, east, south, and west. Start moving

---

1. Some groups fashion medicine wheels that rotate in the opposite direction and/or locate specific qualities in different places. These originate from this group's cultural perceptions or geographical location and are equally correct methods of procedures for them or you.

around your circle, clarifying these issues. Some may not be easy to recognize: it takes time to consciously see the forces at work. Then start looking at what happens to your issue as it moves to its opposite pole. Moving clockwise, walk this circle, over and over and over. Observe the consciousness at work. Define its positions. See where it is too weak or too strong or stuck, and bring it into harmony with what is around it. If you wish, you can further map out your issue multi-dimensionally, using the basic medicine wheel as it spirals up to the center point of spiritual light and down to the center point of inconscient darkness.

You can come back to this form again and again over many sessions. You can also explore the various other symbols we have discussed in this chapter. Another variation to this exercise is to work with a clear *quartz ball. Here you place yourself or your issue at the middle of the sphere. You can feel you are protected inside this universe. The molecular structure of quartz is a double triangle, so it inherently helps balance consciousness.*

Second Perspective: Evolution of Physical Form on Earth

The study of evolution is an examination of consciousness from the feminine perspective of universal energy. It is a study of the upward directed triangle. It is energy that is seeking to grow from gross physical matter back to a state of perfection.

On Earth, a major starting point for the physical development of form is the mineral world, which evolved into plants, animals, and then humans. Each of these levels represents a major step forward in the ability of consciousness to fully act while embedded in solid form. Each level is based on the capacities of the levels preceding it to which it has added new capacities, as Earth existence pursues its endless search for perfection. Each level is also a world of its own with specific issues it is seeking to master, and each has its own direct connection to the source.

In the West, Darwin observed this steady growth in capacity, and called it evolution. He saw this process as a physical one. Many centuries before, an Indian yogi named Kapila studied this process and saw it as an effort by Earth to attain perfection both outwardly and inwardly. He called the effort to attain perfection of form evolution. He called the effort to attain full awareness, or perfection of consciousness, involution.

Let's investigate each segment of Earth life (mineral, animal, and human), in order to more fully comprehend the process that is taking place.

The mineral world is excellent for holding consciousness forms steady. This can either be a physical structure, such as a building, or a consciousness structure such as wisdom.

This is why so many people find that having specific stones around their home or on their body makes them feel very good in specific ways. Different stones embody different types of consciousness; for example, clear quartz embodies balanced energy while amethyst, which is quartz but with manganese added, focuses this balance within the mental spectrum of energy. Stones, however, cannot easily move by themselves and do not adjust well to sudden change, such as temperature or a sharp blow.

Plants are more supple. They can bend with the forces of nature, such as the wind, and naturally grow and change over time. But they are still anchored in one spot, sometimes dependent on external forces even for reproduction. Plants have increased the devotional aspects of the rock kingdom to serve the source's dream of full manifestation in matter. They self-givingly provide the world with such offerings as simplicity and beauty, fragrance, and many kinds of sustenance from food to medicine.

Animals have advanced to free movement. It required tremendous vital determination to take this step and the many types of consciousness that permit a solid form to move on Earth are the dominant forces here. Awareness and self-offering have advanced even more.

The human level has further evolved and includes the capacities of all preceding levels. We can hold like stone; we can adjust and bend with the winds of change like plants; we can move about freely like animals. Added to this is a growing range of awareness and self-offering—consciousness instinctively continuing its inherent drive to perfect its nature and return to the source where true satisfaction resides. When these drives become conscious, progress is more rapid.

Some traditions see life as evolving past the human level to another level, referred to variously as illumined, perfected, Christed, and divine. Traditionally, it has been perceived that there is a very large dividing line between the human and the illumined consciousness. But today, as more and more individuals are passing through this dividing line, we are finding this realm is smoothly connected to the human level and also to all the other levels as well. We are also discovering that there are actually many levels of illumined consciousness through which each human will eventually climb on their way to ultimate union with the source.

According to yogic scientists, evolution is the very purpose and function of life on Earth. Earth is a very special place. It is a plane of existence where life has the opportunity to attain conscious oneness with the source while still existing in solid form. Through a process the yogis call reincarnation, a spark of consciousness moves up through the various stages of Earth development, gradually mastering the lessons of each plane. Once it reaches the human level, it still has hundreds of incarnations to go as it refines its awareness and capacities. There are on Earth at any one time both newly-human beings and old, mature souls. This is similar to children progressing through the same school, one class mastering the ABCs and another learning to put sentences together to write a story.

Everything on Earth is interrelated and involved in this same process. We are all brothers and sisters of spirit, each working in different outer forms or on different steps of the same ladder of progress. Native Americans recognize this, and honor the Great Spirit inside their brother and sister rocks, plants, and animals whom they feel comfortable asking for help in healing or whose self-offering they accept with gratitude when it is necessary to take the plant or animal's life to sustain their own. Christians and Jews recognize this interconnection in their emphasis on stewardship, which ideally means that humans, as perhaps the highest life form, accept the responsibility to protect Earth and all that is on it. The yogic recognition of this interconnectedness of all forms is seen in their practice of ahimsa—non-harm to any living thing.

When a society, or an individual, believes physical objects exist in separate worlds that are not connected with each other, they will not comprehend the ultimate interrelatedness of all existence. They will therefore not mind destroying something they consider to be of lesser value. Western technology has, to date, caused serious problems for the health of our Earth because of this limited matter-based perception.

Exercise 9:
How a Quality Changes as it Evolves

To experience the evolution of consciousness on Earth, we are going to once again work with the consciousness of peace. Since peace is a universal quality, it exists everywhere, at all levels. It is the expression and awareness of peace that changes.

Sit quietly, observe and identify with each level of creation—mineral, plant, animal, human—and watch how the awareness and understanding of peace changes. Don't stop at the ordinary human level: reflect on those beings who represent perfected humanity—the great spiritual figures such as Krishna, Buddha, and Christ. How do they experience peace?

Now look closely at yourself. Whatever you imagine, you embody in some form. You contain inside yourself the whole universe of experiences. The common slang terms we use show that we unconsciously take all levels of consciousness into consideration. Where do you have a "stone-hard consciousness," are "solid as a rock," or are "clear as a crystal"? Where do you "veg out"—slang for sitting still and doing nothing—or "stand as tall and strong as an oak tree"? Where do you have "animal passions" or are "faithful as a dog"? Where are you "all-too-human" or repre-

sent *"the best qualities of humanity"? Where do you embody light—are "totally divine" or "a real angel" or "truly spiritual"?*

Contemplate how you can personally evolve in your capacity to embody peace by bringing the stone, plant, animal, and human levels of awareness—all inside yourself—into the light. How does doing this help our Earth consciousness collectively evolve forward as well?

The Third Perspective: Inner Development of Earth Consciousness

This perspective looks at consciousness as it moves from the one inner source to the multiplicity of forms on Earth. It looks at consciousness from the perspective of the downward flowing, masculine creator triangle. The previous section explored the opposite movement, starting from the upward flowing, feminine creation triangle.

In scientifically charting the descent of consciousness, we are observing one substance which has split itself into different qualities, or aspects, of its own universal nature. For clarity and simplicity, we will concentrate on what consciousness looks like as it becomes human form.

Yogis see consciousness as entering the human body through seven major vortexes or energy centers, called chakras. All sacred sciences observe this embodiment of spirit, although they may use different terms.

We will start from the highest level of consciousness and chart its descent. To help you understand this process, we will be comparing the embodiment of universal consciousness to the process light experiences when it passes through a prism.

When clear light passes through a prism, it separates into its individual components, each of which has its own qualities—color, vibratory rate, sound, etc. Light separates into seven basic bands of colors, arranged on either side of the point of emission from the prism: red, orange, yellow, green, blue, purple, and clear shimmering, with other subtle colors existing beyond the current range of ordinary perception. Each color comes from the same source and is still connected to that source, yet manifests its own specialized quality. Our body functions as a prism for universal light to act in different ways.

1. Universal Unmanifest Consciousness

This is the consciousness that exists forever—before time and form begins and after it ends. All existence is made up of this field and is forever within this field. Universal consciousness is infinite, eternal, omnipresent, omniscient, and omnipotent. While this field is beyond name, we attempt to describe it with such terms as God, Mind, Void, Chaos, the

Supreme, the source, light, consciousness, energy, and so on. This field can be understood as full-spectrum light before it enters the dividing process of the prism.

2. Individualized Consciousness

Here universal unmanifest consciousness begins to shape itself into the forms of creation. The first step is spinning off a portion of itself: individualizing its universal consciousness in some way. Some of these particles of consciousness will go on to become rocks or plants, chairs or tables, and a plethora of forms and beings in many different dimensions.

Once the source launches a spark of its own existence into this game we call life, the spark begins its own game: its own rich and varied process of growth. If it is a simple spark of existence, it may exist at first in a group with other sparks and together they create a simple form. When the form it is participating in stops existing, through death or destruction, it may simply detach from the whole and go back into the universal consciousness. But it has acquired some experience in how to sustain its existence inside the realm of matter.

Gradually, over time, a spark of consciousness may grow in maturity. In our dimension, some grow large enough and strong enough to exist as the soul around which a plant or animal or other more complex life form assembles itself. By the time the spark has grown into a soul around which a human being takes shape, it is already quite advanced. Yet it still has innumerable incarnations to go before it achieves its full potential, which is to consciously partake of the same perfection that is the ultimate source. Only a few very great souls have attained this goal: they are the Buddhas, Krishnas, and Christs of our planet. Once souls attain this state of awareness, they exist as a pervasive, perfected consciousness that has evolved within our world, thoroughly knows its ways, and acts now as a partner with the unmanifest source in its activities on Earth. These perfected beings are our older brothers and sisters and we can call on them for assistance in our own efforts.

In a human being, this second plane is analogous to a prism. A prism takes undifferentiated light and separates it into specific colors and energies. The soul receives the light of the Supreme and manifests it through very specific planes of consciousness. The levels we describe next (illustrated in Fig. 4) are manifestations of consciousness as specific frequency bands. Each has a definite energy, color, sound, and function.

3. The Heart/Psychic Realm

The seat of the soul in the human body is deep inside the heart chakra. The yogic symbol for the heart chakra is shown on the left. We have already seen that this signifies the harmonious balancing

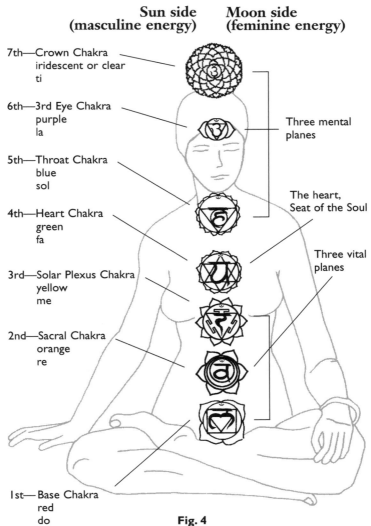

Sun side
(masculine energy)

Moon side
(feminine energy)

7th—Crown Chakra
iridescent or clear
ti

6th—3rd Eye Chakra
purple
la

Three mental
planes

5th—Throat Chakra
blue
sol

4th—Heart Chakra
green
fa

The heart,
Seat of the Soul

3rd—Solar Plexus Chakra
yellow
me

Three vital
planes

2nd—Sacral Chakra
orange
re

1st— Base Chakra
red
do

Fig. 4
The 7 Chakra System

of all issues. The heart chakra is the pivotal point in the human body. It is the fulcrum that loves and balances the needs of the inner world of spirit with the outer world of matter.

The heart is at the center of the medicine wheel of our lives. Inside it is the source. To its north—the heart to the head—are the mental realms and the three higher chakra levels. South of it—the heart to the base of the trunk— are the emotional realms and the three lower chakra levels. East of it—the right side of the body—are the warm yang issues of life and west of it—the left side of the body—are the cool yin issues of life.

The primary color of the heart chakra is green—the color of growth. Pink, the color of compassionate love, is also present. The heart chakra's sound, on the Western musical scale, is the central note, *fa*.

4. The Mind

The function of the mind is to help the soul and heart bring order to the chaos of options available in the universe. It offers a human being the power to discriminate, order, and choose. The mind operates through the three higher, or northern, chakras.

The seventh chakra is the crown chakra, located at the very top of the head. It is directly connected with universal knowledge. If you have ever looked inside a quartz crystal and seen a rainbow, this spectrum of color is similar to the color associated with the crown chakra. The sound of this chakra is *ti*.

The crown chakra is called by yogis the thousand-petaled lotus because it contains all colors and sounds as separate petals. When the flower of this chakra is fully open, these petals exist together harmoniously in a state of total clarity. Some disciplines see the crown chakra as tinged with purple or blue and see translucent clarity existing at another chakra point above the head.

The sixth chakra is the third eye, located just below the middle of the forehead and above and between our outer physical eyes. It offers inner wisdom and clarity of inner sight. Its color is an amethyst purple—some people see an indigo blue/purple—and its sound is *la*.

The fifth chakra is located in the middle of the throat. It offers the ability to communicate the inner knowledge to the outer world. Its color is blue, seen as either an indigo blue (the color of lapis lazuli), a turquoise green-blue, or a sky blue (the color of blue lace agate). Its sound is *sol*.

5. *The Vital Plane (Emotions)*

This plane controls energy and emotions and, when funneled into the human body, adds action to the loving heart plane and thinking mental realms. It operates through the three lower, or southern, chakras. At lower levels of awareness, humans often confuse true love (which comes from the heart) with the carnal passions and emotions of this energetic, protective, and reproductive realm.

The third chakra is the solar plexus, which deals with personal power and identity. Personal magnetism comes from here. The solar plexus chakra is yellow in color and has the sound of *mi*—or "me."

The second chakra is the sacral chakra, located below the navel. It deals with relationships with others, with issues of community, and with creative and sensual instincts from the carnal to mystical levels. Its color is orange and its sound is *re*.

The first chakra is located at the base of the trunk of the body between the sexual organs and the anus, and relates to basic survival instincts and our relationship with the universe. Its color is red and its sound is *do*.

Some disciplines associate the red-orange color with the second chakra and red-black or black with the first chakra.

Some disciplines use an extended chakra system of eleven, thirteen, or fifteen vortexes. There are actually thousands of chakras associated with the human body, including chakras on the tip of each finger. Besides energy vortexes, the human body is also composed of many over-lapping energy grids.

6. The Physical Plane
(The Body or Solid Material Form)
All qualities of the above planes cannot be put to work on

the solid earth plane if they are not housed in a solid physical form. The gross physical plane gives the qualities of the preceding planes a home. This is the function of the human body with its hands, eyes, knees, feet, and so on. Here colors often combine to form dense, earthy red-browns, dark forest greens, or midnight blues, and their sound is a low cacophonous drone, or a beautiful orchestra, combining all the other sounds. We call spiritual masters *enlightened* because they have mastered all these planes and thus work with tremendous clarity on the physical plane: the pure light of the source is seen brightly shining inside of their physical forms. Each enlightened human being has an individual crystal-clear color and sound, because they have focused universal consciousness in a very specific way.

7. *Inconscient Matter*
(Total, Inert Density of Consciousness)

This plane lies beneath all the other layers of consciousness. It is the dark polarity that defines how bright light can be. Molecules of light/consciousness/energy are so densely compacted here that no movement is possible. It is deeper than the rock consciousness; it is blacker than the black holes of space; it is darker than the lowest regions of what some disciplines call Hell. Here color and sound are compressed so tightly that it appears absent altogether: a total blackout. It is the ultimate state of physicality.

Exercise 10:
The Quality of Peace as it Descends Through the Planes of Consciousness

In Exercise 9 we observed the quality of peace as it evolved through the material forms of our world. Now we shall look at peace as it descends from the source into the world.

Let's start by considering the universal aspect of peace, which inherently includes all inside itself, but has no form in which to act. Watch it descend through the planes of consciousness. Each new level requires it to accept a more restricted consciousness but also provides it with a more powerful means to act on Earth.

So, in a positive way, consider how the universal quality of peace expands its ability to manifest itself as it descends through the planes of the soul, heart, mind, vital, and physical. How does it change on the higher and lower levels of each plane? How rich and varied is this peace when we combine all the ways together?

Focus on some part of your life in which you wish to more fully experience peace. First look at how each separate plane and chakra can beneficially contribute its qualities to that state. Now observe how, through peaceful cooperation, each plane and chakra supports and strengthens each other. State your intent to put this new awareness into practice, and call on the assistance of your chosen guide to help you. Begin manifesting this in your life even as you move out of your meditation. Return to this exercise often, to gain further insights and to reinforce the quality of peace inside yourself.

Points to Ponder

The planes of consciousness descend from the creator's side of the triangle while the outer evolutionary development of Earth forms ascends from the creation's side of the triangle. As each side progresses, it manifests more and more aspects of its potentials and is also gradually interacting more and more with the core forces of its polar opposite. This is why Earth is such a powerful yet complex arena: all forces are in play, in different ways. Ultimately, to solve the puzzle of creator/creation, light/darkness, we must move beyond the polarities to the one common source.

At birth, when a soul enters the physical plane, it has descended through so many planes of consciousness that it has lost sight of its source. The nature of this descent is like passing through a series of veils; each is semi-transparent but, when overlaid on each other, they gradually obscure the source. Young children sometimes remember details of the worlds behind the veils, but slowly forget as they focus on the difficulties of mastering the physical: moving, speaking, and meeting their needs and wants.

Children gradually adjust to the society around them and either accept its perceptions or fight them.

Difficulties stimulate people to reach for survival solutions. Very few people search for God, or source, when they are in a pleasurable state. However, in this new age of spiritual awareness, the process is changing. We are learning, as a way of life, how to consciously go to our own body, vital, mind, heart, and soul for assistance in achieving our objectives. We are learning to respect the wisdom of the soul, the love of the heart, the organizing capacities of the mind, the dynamism of the vital, and the form of the body. As more and more of us master this understanding, the collective expression of this awareness—society—is itself being transformed. A larger organism reflects the development level of its individual parts. We are in the midst of our own Hundredth Monkey experience.

However, actually mastering consciousness is still a difficult skill that the soul must learn over many lifetimes. Thus, human beings sometimes focus on mastering a particular plane in a particular lifetime. Philosophers, for example, are interested primarily in the mental plane, while athletes are mostly interested in the physical plane. As the reincarnating soul matures and selects different life experiences for itself, it gradually strengthens its inherent wisdom and understanding of all the planes.

Yogis call people who have attained the level of full mastery of consciousness God-realized or self-realized, referring to different perspectives of the same state. God-realized human beings are those who have completed the graduate level of their personal work. Some now wish only to merge with the source and not return to Earth. Others wish to remain in the Earth arena but help from the inner realms. This group includes the bodhisattvas, and some saints and spiritual masters of all traditions. God-realization is an evolving, progressive state and there are many levels to the process, with some individuals choosing to evolve farther than others. Sri Chinmoy describes these additional states of God-realization as God-revelation and God-manifestation. God-revelation is the capacity of individuals to reveal the word and nature of God to others. God-manifestation is the ability of people to actually bring to Earth, through their own body, the pure light of the source. If approached sequentially, Sri Chinmoy tells us, God-manifestation is even more difficult to attain than God-realization. He advocates a new approach in which individuals seek to balance the very high polarities of God-realization and God-manifestation as they progress. Instead of withdrawing from society to search for God in the solitude of a cave, ashram, or monastery, his students are asked to balance the pursuit of the highest inner goal with the serving of humanity in a soulful manner.

Exercise 11:
Experiencing the Movement of Consciousness
Through Sound

According to yoga, the Sanskrit word AUM is the original seed sound of the universe, and the point at which manifestation begins. AUM is a mantra, which is the embodiment in sound of a specific consciousness/energy, just as yantras and mandalas are the embodiment in visual form of consciousness/energy. The Sri Yantra Mandala (see page 67) is the visual counterpart of AUM. The Biblical statement "In the beginning was the Word" refers to this initial sound and the Christian "amen" reflects this sound. "One," a chant used by some cynical physical scientists to show the power of any sound, works because it represents in the English language much the same resonance and concept as AUM.

AUM is three separate energies acting as one. It is therefore chanted as three separate parts. A is the creating of form, U is the sustaining of form, and M is the dissolution of form. By repeating this chant over and over, you experience the cyclic nature of existence: as one form ends, another form comes into existence, is sustained for a while and then begins to disintegrate, and so on. Yogis use this chant to aid their awareness of the universal nature of existence. By lengthening the chanting of one of the three parts, they can focus on bringing its particular consciousness more strongly into their lives.

Chanting AUM out loud, powerfully and fast, clears the gross physical. Chanting it inwardly, slowly, softly, and sweetly, calms the higher senses. You can visualize any of the chakras and chant it from that place, to clear and strengthen its positive qualities. When doing this, chant AUM in the musical note associated with that particular chakra.

Chanting a prayer, tone, or phrase repeatedly is one way all traditions help their practitioners identify with, memorize, and know well that particular object or consciousness. This can be multiplication tables chanted by school children; or the 108 names of God in the Far Eastern faiths. To help focus concentration and keep count, most spiritual disciplines eventually move on from using simple tools such as pebbles or grains of rice to creating some type of counting device that also has symbolic meaning; these are called rosaries, malas, or prayer beads.

Right now let's chant A-U-M inside your heart chakra. This will help you calm and strengthen this key consciousness point. Please chant AUM using the heart's musical note of "fa." Using any counting device you have around, do one hundred repetitions of this sound, loud or soft, aloud or inwardly, according to your inclination. Your chanting should be conscious, not mechanical. Focus initially on separating the three parts of the sound, making them equal in duration, so that you include their individual energies.

When you have finished, sit in silent meditation and feel the vibrating peace inside yourself.

If you like this feeling, you can expand on its potentials. The following eleven-day traditional yogic exercise, if completed, will significantly clarify, purify, and bring peace into your consciousness. Using a mala, which has 108 beads (or any similar counting device with its cycle of numbers), chant AUM once on each bead and do this six times, called "rounds." The next day do this seven rounds, and so on up to eleven rounds, then work your way back down again to the six rounds. The yogis call this chanting of rounds doing "japa."

3

The Personal Factor

"Who am I?"

Since time immemorial, humanity has pondered this question of questions. The greatest sages say this is the only question worth asking and that the process of answering this question will take you to the ultimate goal, the source of the universe itself.

When some people are asked "Who am I?" they respond by saying they are the body: eyes, nose, arms, legs. Some feel they are defined by what they do: husband, wife, parent, executive, professional athlete, dishwasher. Some respond in psychological terms; others in philosophical, ecological, political, philosophical, or spiritual terms. All are equally true. And yet each is only another aspect of a person's full reality.

Here we are going to show you some ways to perceive of yourself from a consciousness perspective. There are many schools of thought about this subject for it is the main motivating force in our lives. Whatever you know now, and wherever you perceive from now, is all right. We only wish to extend this knowledge to further your own growth, by whatever process you prefer. The following story shows the energetic truth behind this statement.

In South India, in the first half of the twentieth century, two very great yogis lived within half a day's walk of each other. One of these yogis was Sri Aurobindo. He was a Bengali visionary trained at Cambridge University who eventually devoted his life to the exploration of consciousness, especially to the higher levels of the mind that humanity as a whole has not yet tapped. He wrote many books that explored his revolutionary discoveries about the nature of consciousness. He devoted his life to understanding human nature in all its most subtle, spiritually scientific ramifications.

Another equally revered yogi, Sri Ramana Maharshi, lived unclothed in a cave. He had no formal education. He wrote nothing. He dedicated himself to understanding life by asking and answering what he believed was the only one question worth exploring: "Who am I?"

These two men, starting from radically different perspectives, methods, and personality types, came to similar realizations. Each personally experienced himself as the embodiment of God in form.

How you answer "Who am I?" is anchored in your perspective of life. It can be approached from the polarity of all-inclusiveness: I am the mind *and* the body; I am the secretary *and* the mother—or the football player *and* the brother—and so on, until you know yourself to be the all-inclusive source of the universe. It can also be approached from the polarity of "neti-neti"—"not this, not that"—which means, upon exploring, an individual finds I am *not* the mind, I am *not* the body, I am *not* a secretary or a football player, because if I eliminate these experiences, I still exist. I am, therefore, something else. By continually eliminating the illusions of existence, the seeker gradually moves back to perceiving themself as the original source of the universe, which is the same point as the opposite approach also achieved. The source is one, and all roads lead to it.

Let's start by focusing on what you currently perceive yourself to be. When you have finished the following exercise, write down your current perceptions. After a month of practicing meditation, write down your new perceptions. Continue doing this, every six months, and over the years you will be surprised at how your perception has changed.

Exercise 12:
Who Am I?

Sit at your shrine and calm and center yourself. Ask "Who am I?" Sit silently in meditation and enter into the experience of who you have assumed you are.

Now let's start expanding your perceptions. We have already discussed the following viewpoints: all-inclusiveness, neti-neti, Sri Aurobindo's intellectual approach, Sri Ramana Maharshi's devotional approach, perceiving yourself (Chapter 2) as the body, vital, mind, heart, soul, or as the embodied eternal source of the universe.

Select one of these viewpoints to explore right now. Enter fully into the experience of the viewpoint you have selected. When you have reached an awareness that you are comfortable with, stop your exploration and experience that awareness. Fully explore what this new awareness means for your life. Envision how you will incorporate this in your everyday life.

Come out of your meditation session.

You should repeat this exercise often, for every time you reach deeper or higher into yourself, it opens up entire new vistas that warrant further exploration. You can stay with one approach, or try various approaches and see the different perceptions you acquire.

Five Different Ways To Know Consciousness

Some people learn best through the physical act of doing, others by mentally conceptualizing, and still others by working to maintain a loving consciousness no matter what happens to them. Each of us learns in a slightly different manner and feels most comfortable approaching life by a very personal combination of methods. Classic yogic science has defined five distinctly different approaches, and over the centuries whole schools for the application of this knowledge have evolved. Most of us today combine various elements of these approaches in our lives. You can study the following distinctions to further comprehend where you fit in your own consciousness orientation.

Hatha yoga is the yoga of physical discipline. It is progress through mastery of the physical body. It includes the study and energetic strengthening of bodily structure and such subtle body sciences as pranayama (breath control) practiced in Exercise 5.

Karma yoga is the yoga of action. It is progress through sanctifying the performance of any task or job, no matter what it is, to the source.

Jnana yoga is the yoga of knowledge. It seeks to fully comprehend and understand how the universe works. This is known as a long and slow path because of the infinite nature of knowledge itself. Most philosophers belong to this category.

Bhakti yoga is the path of love, devotion, and surrender to the person of the Lord Beloved Supreme. This is the fastest, simplest, most personal, and most direct of all the yogas. It teaches that nothing surpasses the direct experience of union with the source of all existence.

Raja yoga is the yoga of kings and leaders. It is progress through the mastery of all the yogas combined. The original function of leaders was to hold the combined political, spiritual, and governing dreams and ideals of their people. They needed to be strong (hatha yoga) and to act (karma yoga) through wisdom (jnana yoga) and devotion (bhakti yoga).

We are extremely fortunate, in America, to be the juncture point for all the cultures of the world. The presence of the United Nations on American soil represents, in the solid physical form, the oneness of spirit that American culture at its best offers to the world. I was fortunate enough to work at the United Nations for seven years. During this time I saw and experienced firsthand the profound efforts of many different cultural systems to understand and cooperate with each other. This came down to basic personal interactions within departments, which, in my case, included individuals from twenty different countries, with many different native languages and social preconceptions. I observed not only how difficult energetic adjustments can be, but also how trapped we can become if we hold on to belief systems that tell us there is only one way to navigate through energy and achieve our goals. At the United Nations, we learned to respond by identification with other systems of thought. This was a healthy, consciousness-expanding experience.

We need to do this in the realm of consciousness studies as well. All religions, philosophies, and disciplines contain part of the truth but not the full truth; no one and no thing can fully encompass infinity, eternity, and immortality. If we will cooperate, learn from, and share with each other, we can make tremendous advances in our knowledge.

In today's globalizing and consciousness-expanding society, whatever our current base, we are being required to expand beyond it. The old ways no longer work and so we must keep expanding our perceptions to survive. Moreover, we are moving into an era where the dividing lines between matter and the higher consciousness dimensions are softening and disappearing. Energy workers are developing the capacity to look directly into consciousness structures and see how they move and why. Things we humans once had to take on faith, as told to us by great visionaries, we are now able to see for ourselves.

Different energy workers have the capacity to see different things. The same is true with you. You need to find your own methods to achieve your goals. To show you the range of options available, I'd like to share with you some basic information about three workers I especially admire: Starr Fuentes, Anna Hayes, and Sri Chinmoy. Each has followed their own truth and has directly perceived consciousness from very different perspectives. Each is contributing significantly to society, in very different ways.

Starr Fuentes would be classified as a karma yogi, because her hands-on work as a classical American faith healer, a medicine woman, and an energy scientist is her spiritual orientation. America's Eurocentric culture does not have a strong tradition of energy healing to learn from. Those of us working in the field today have had to rely on intuition and assistance from a wide variety of inner and outer guides. This is true of Starr as well. From this base, however, she has travelled around the world to acquire information on subtle healing techniques. Because of language differences, she could not communicate verbally with many of these teachers. But they could understand each other very well in the communication of energy methods, procedures, and capacities. Starr has worked hard to scientifically comprehend and order her healing knowledge into an empirically verifiable and reproducible body of information.

Like much of the energy education that has gone on since ancient times, the knowledge of how to actually work with consciousness is a science best transmitted from teacher to student, on an experiential level. Once the teacher shows you how to enter into and work with these energies, you have received the energy knowledge to do it for yourself.

Starr now focuses on training other Americans how to consciously develop their own capacities. According to Starr there are different types of subtle energy that assist in the healing of body, mind, and spirit. She states that:

Healing energy is composed of five forces. Some people become great healers because they have mastered healing with the dominant force that their own body runs with. Most people cannot become powerful healers because they attempt to use a force other than the one that flows through them.

She explains that each of us first needs to understand how we intuitively work with energy. Once this is perceived, we can move on to master the other ways as well. She defines these five forces:

Plast. This force uses the plasma flows inside and outside of the body to correct plasma and ectoplasma in others.

Wila. Wila uses the power of chi and electromagnetic thoughtforms to change the form of the disease.

Mag. Mag is an eraser-type force that returns energies to their original blueprint.

Sap. Sap is a force that uses nature to drain a disease from the body.

Noa. Noa is a force that goes between worlds and time
to uncreate the energies of the original cause of the disease.[1]

Anna Hayes approaches her work with consciousness from a jnana yoga perspective and is part of the Melchizedek traditions. She is the youngest of the three — in her early thirties — yet she has been studying in her field for over twenty-seven years. She is part of a new group of energy workers who openly state they are learning in part from meta-terrestrial beings — beings from the higher levels of what she describes as our own fifteen-dimensional universe. Anna is continually learning from these beings, receiving information from them about an advanced science of consciousness called Keylonta. This science uses geometric forms as a communication language.

Anna works to coalesce and integrate the voluminous amount of information she receives from these subtle beings with her own experiences in these subtle dimensions. She is able to energetically connect people to these meta-terrestrial energies, to facilitate the individual's spiritual and consciousness growth.

Anna's information fills several books, with more on the way. She uses many scientific schematics to show how consciousness progresses, in an orderly and scientific

1. Starr Fuentes. From class materials, copyright 1999.

manner, up through fifteen dimensions, from the gross physical through the subtle body, the spiritual body, and into a state of ante-matter—conscious awareness before it is embodied in form. She is able to show concretely many of the ways energy coalesces into specific functional patterns, including geometric forms, overlapping grids, multiple chakras, and energy nodules.

Anna has also diagrammed how our individual strengths and weaknesses and various abilities are clearly encoded in our DNA structure. She uses a schematic that describes DNA as it moves into the realms of subtle energy. Our current scientific instruments can only record two DNA strands. Her more subtle methods of study have graphed twelve paired electric and magnetic strands, each dealing with a specific aspect of consciousness, and each composed of numerous nodule points that control specific functions in our energetic existence.

Anna believes that science and spirit should be inextricably one and the same. She acknowledges the difficulty of working with the complex structures she presents and emphasizes the value of spiritual focus to cut through the scientific mechanics and simply connect with higher energies. These energies can, by their mere presence, clear these blockages for you.

Sri Chinmoy is a proponent of bhakti yoga—love, devotion, and surrender to the Supreme. He was raised in

India, lived through the struggle for Indian independence, and studied yoga at the Sri Aurobindo Ashram. He was one of the first Eastern gurus to come to the West. He arrived in New York in 1964 and has taught from there ever since.

Sri Chinmoy feels the human mission is to attain the goal—oneness with the source—and the more direct and speedily it can take place, the better. The mind, Sri Chinmoy feels, only gets in the way of this process. There is always another "why" to be answered. So he urges his students to reduce their lives to the barest, simplest essentials and to live, like a child, in the heart. This is not, however, as easy as it would seem, for there are many obstacles in the way. Most of us have lives filled with self-created complexities that obstruct such a profoundly simple lifestyle.

Sri Chinmoy has the marvelous capacity to make the most complex concepts very simple and direct experiences. What follows is an alphabetical list of qualities that he recommends every human being cultivate for personal progress.

Aspiration. This is the unquenchable fire that burns inside of you and consumes all obstacles that stand between you and your goal. It is essential, for a sincere seeker, as you will encounter many obstacles along your journey to the source.

Detachment. When you begin your inner explorations,

you soon learn that you can affect the outcome by your desire to achieve a particular result. To achieve accurate results, you must detach yourself from your desires regarding that subject and work in a clear and open inner space. Detachment and desirelessness are highly valued in traditional sacred societies that are seeking to travel rapidly from the human condition to the divine consciousness.

Determination is your commitment to reach your own personal truth, no matter what obstacles are put in your way.

Gratitude is your conscious appreciation of the assistance other aspects of the same one source are extending to help you achieve your goals.

Hope is essential to the inner journey. If you lose hope that you can achieve your goal, you stop trying very soon. If you see yourself losing hope, you must consciously do all you can to restore it to your energy system.

Love, devotion, and surrender are considered by bhakti yogis as the three most important qualities to cultivate if you are seeking to establish personal contact with the source. Many religions and many spiritual groups approach the inner worlds from this point of view.

Surrender is a misunderstood word in the West, where we have fought so hard for personal freedom. In the spiritual realms, surrender has positive connotations; it's a form of identification with a higher consciousness. Through the surrender of everything in your life to the all-encompassing, all-light source, anything that is not of the source is burned away or falls behind. Surrender, for those individuals so inclined, is a very rapid means to remove obstructions and to fly directly to the source, their Absolute Beloved Lord Supreme.

Persistence means never giving up. No matter how many mistakes you make, no matter how many times you have to start over, no matter how many obstacles you encounter, you must never give up. Whatever forces are in your way eventually have to bow to your aspiration, determination, and persistence.

Purity is necessary if you wish to travel into the very highest levels of consciousness. These levels are far above human desires, which keep us bound to the flesh. Purity has different connotations in different studies. To some it means simplicity and at the far extreme it entails a monk's life of celibacy.

Intent

No matter which way you choose to explore consciousness, perhaps the most critical personal ingredient is your intent. Intent is your inner compass pointing the way forward; it determines the direction you go and the help you accept to get there. You should take great care in establishing the intent of your actions. For while the first step forward on a path is small, you are choosing to proceed in a specific direction that is going to become more and more individualistic over time.

Your intent in one area of your life gradually affects the nature of your decisions in all other areas of your life. For example, an individual whose intent is to become a materially rich person will choose different forces to work with than will a person whose primary intent is to become a spiritually rich person.

Intent is a personal decision that focuses your awareness on the who, what, where, why, when, and how of a specific issue. Intent is especially powerful at those critical juncture points when you are making some change in your life. In Hinduism, this period of change is recognized as such an important aspect of the universal flow of consciousness that it has its own god, or cosmic force, Siva. Siva is the energy inside transformation and change and is part of a triumvirate of cosmic forces, the others being Brahma (the creator force) and Vishnu (the sustainer and protector of life).

Group Intent

When you join a particular group, you agree to accept their collective intent. This intent has been shaped out of the group's collective consciousness, which has gradually agreed to approach the issues of life from a certain perspective. This agreement evolves, over time, into complex interconnected and self-supporting patterns (much like the Sri Yantra Mandala). Decisions that may seem strange to an outsider can be understood when the group's particular pattern is discerned. Creating change involves altering these energy patterns in some way, either peacefully or violently.

Part of the function of childhood is to train your being's consciousness structure to resonate with the specific perceptual system, or intent structure, into which you have been born. At first you learn this from your caregivers (usually parents) and later from schools and social groups. Inside this realm you select your own personal intent, or location. Each specific task you perform also has its own intent, or resonance. The descent of these intents, energetically, looks much like the Sri Yantra Mandala we discussed in Chapter 2. From a single core form, all other forms spin out, in descending sequence.

Various energy disciplines term the places where these energies interconnect "assemblage points." This is a visual, and accurate, description of the energies involved.

An assemblage point is a location within the human energy field at which separate lines of energy meet. It is that point at which various consciousness capacities gather together to perform a specific function. There are major and minor assemblage points; each has traveled over a series of connecting points to meet a specific purpose.

Assemblage points work in a manner similar to an electric power grid. These grids take energy from a main source and step it down through a series of transformers (assemblage points) to finally enter a home, room, and appliance (your body and the specific function you are going to work with). When an energy grid breaks down or malfunctions, it needs to be fixed, have new fuses put in, or be rewired, and the same is true with the human energy machine, your body.

Assemblage points can be at various levels of the heart, mind, vital, at some point in the subtle body field a greater distance out from the physical, or even at a point outside the parameters of the personal energy field itself. Different people and groups have learned from their own members how to locate these lines at particular spots (the Hundredth Monkey Principle). This means they have learned how to step down cosmic energy in a particular way for a specific function. Although each group knows a correct way home, the routes may be different from each other.

Energy workers very quickly learn that they can consciously shift their energetic assemblage points and move into different realities. Some Westerners do this unconsciously, such as actors when they play different roles and individuals who "fit in" wherever they go, whether it is talking with construction workers or heads of state. Shamans and occultists consciously manipulate assemblage points for energetic purposes including inner travel to acquire powers and assistance from other dimensions. Some are so facile they can even change their bodily form. Examples of such shape shifting include wizards such as Merlin of the King Arthur tales and the legendary Native American Crow women who could change into fish, birds, bears, and so on. Some Indian yogis and Buddhist ascetics can also do this, as well as travel through time and space.

Energy workers and masters of consciousness can use this knowledge to assist themselves and others. For example, during World War I many soldiers on the battlefields of Europe saw a kindly man with a long white beard appear before them to inspire and provide protection. Only years later did some of these people come across a picture and recognize their protector as the yogi Sri Aurobindo. Although he lived thousands of miles away in India, Sri Aurobindo was able to inwardly travel to assist individuals who, when they intensely asked for protection, unconsciously connected to his world of consciousness. This is what happens to all of us when we powerfully ask for assistance: we resonantly connect to a specific realm of the inner worlds.

When your intent is to change some aspect of your life, what you are actually doing is working to rewire your energy in a new way. This is similar to deciding to rewire your den to handle the needs of your new computer system. Change is often difficult to accomplish, for our energetic lines are wired into a series of assemblage points that step up in power to join larger energy grids. Making successful change requires finding the key assemblage point in your energy system. This requires being able to walk through the consciousness systems of your life.

In the past, spiritual seekers often left secular society to join a monastic group. They were breaking with the resonant assemblage points locking them into the intent of their outer society and establishing new consciousness paths linking them into the intent of their spiritual group.

There are many ways to understand and work with assemblage points, intent, and consciousness. All focus on the awareness that form is composed of consciousness, or energy, and that form is affected by changes in energy. This knowledge has many practical applications from personal transformation to health issues to managing social and political change.

Exercise 13:
Working with Intent

In meditation, select a situation you are involved in that is giving you cause for concern. Ask yourself what route through consciousness you have taken to set this up in your life. At what level of your personal energy assemblage do you need to make a change to correct this situation? Do you need to ask for help from experts? Who? How will they help you to change this particular situation? Ask the consciousness you are working with at your shrine to help you move forward with these changes. These experts of consciousness are there to help you, but through the universal divine laws of free will they can only do so if you request their assistance.

Moving Into Action

Exploring consciousness is an exciting and fulfilling task. It takes you into the inner realms of existence. As you are discovering, these realms are just as real and active as the outer world you see around you each day. Yogis refer to their work as dealing with the inner worlds (spirit, energy, consciousness) and the outer world (the subtle to gross physical levels of matter). Creating a link between these realms, so that the two worlds flow smoothly together is one of their goals. One method most reflective groups incorporate into their disciplines is a walking or moving meditation. This is a soft, gentle, benign method to link up the two worlds. Groups that participate in this type of activity include the Sufi whirling dervishes, the Christian Labyrinth walkers, and the walking meditations of Zen disciplines. Sustaining this awareness under more energetically active situations is the purpose of the long distance running of the Japanese Buddhist monks, the North and South American Indians, and the Sri Chinmoy

Centre. The Sri Chinmoy Marathon Team even holds a bi-annual Peace Run for the purpose of grounding the consciousness of peace on Earth. This relay passes through over 100 countries, many warring with their neighbors, and invites all people to pause and carry for a brief moment the flaming torch of peace. The relay's mottoes are: "Peace begins with one step" and "Peace begins with you."

Exercise 14:
Moving Meditation

In this exercise, you are going to work to bring one of the qualities mentioned in this chapter from the inner world of consciousness into physical reality. You are going to focus on maintaining a specific consciousness while in motion.

Select your quality, enter into the meditative state, and study what this quality looks like energetically. See how it connects both up and down in your life, from spirit to matter. What do you need to do to anchor this spiritual quality in the physical realm? Focus on that awareness.

Now quietly stand up and peacefully walk about your shrine area, all the while focusing on bringing down this quality into your physical body. It may be more difficult than you thought. Inner forces often seem to fly away, like a bird in flight, once you begin moving about. This is a graphic demonstration of why some beginning meditators feel the science is all right, but definitely not strong enough to meet their everyday needs. You are now practicing making this a practical process.

Mastering the ability to completely connect spirit and matter occurs only at the highest level of expertise. Progress comes one step at a time. So start now. The next steps depend upon your own capacity and receptivity to this activity as it relates to the quality you are seeking to master. You will succeed more rapidly with some qualities than with others and that is all right. A scientist of any kind knows that an experiment must be replicated many times before one discovers just how to attain the goal. You are entering this process right now.

While walking, observe how the quality you have selected shifts when it is grounded in physical action. If the feeling slips away, go back to practicing one of our previous exercises, such as pranayama or chanting the name of the quality, only do it now while you're walking. Next, in this session or a future one, expand this practice by going outside your shrine area. First walk around your yard or in a quiet park-like setting. Practice maintaining the feeling while walking slowly, then quickly. Keep extending this exercise, working to maintain the consciousness while moving along crowded streets, at work, and in every stressful situation of your life.

Running meditations are an excellent way to more fully ground higher planes of consciousness in the body. Here you *are bringing strong, vital power to the process. Working up to distance running is excellent training for bringing positive energies into the body because you cannot succeed at this activity without learning to think and feel positively. Negative thinking and feeling cuts you off from the source of potentially energizing universal consciousness, which you need to draw on to sustain this particular sport. You can begin this energetic process by running half a block and gradually working your way up.*

There is the story of a tourist in New York City who stops a musician on the street and asks, "How do you get to Carnegie Hall?" The musician looks him straight in the eye and responds, "Practice!"

Practice is the key to success in any endeavor. But if you bang away at an old, out-of-tune piano with no teacher, your learning will be slow and difficult. The proper tools and teachers are a great boon. We will cover these issues in the next two chapters.

Tools for Working with Consciousness

The function of this chapter is to acquaint you with various tools for working with consciousness. This chapter will be like going to carpentry school, where you learn how to use tools like a lathe, a burnisher, a soldering torch, and so on. As you learn about the tools of consciousness, you will also learn various ways different energy workers use them. These include strengthening your self physically, mentally, and spiritually, and serving society. What you personally choose to do with these tools, and what further study you choose, is up to you. You are the carpenter building your own life story.

Resonance Tools

If you have ever turned on a fluorescent light and watched

it flicker, you know what happens when energy does not resonate properly. When the connection is not firm, energy does not flow freely. The energy that comes from a broad source and should be stepped down through a transformer does not flow properly. If you want light, you have to find a way to correct the incomplete, blocked flow of energy.

One way consciousness works is through *resonance*. Resonance is what happens when a struck sound oscillates between its two extreme points (its polarities) and these oscillations move forward through time and space. You can understand this by thinking of how electricity is conducted by oscillations along electrical lines to its destination.

Sympathetic resonance can be created in one object by creating a sound in a similar object. For example, if you place two violins next to each other, and then pluck a string on one, the same string on the other violin will start to sympathetically vibrate.

Some of the West's new subtle energy disciplines make use of the principles of resonance to *clear* different parts of our energy system, either of injuries or of the general accumulated debris that comes with life. These disciplines encourage a specific part of our system to recalibrate itself through identification with its ideally healthy resonance. You can affect your own energy system through work with resonance, including identifying with and entering into a specific aspect of consciousness that you admire in a spiritual person or quality.

Resonance pervades every plane of consciousness and every life form. Each function in life has its own resonance. Sounds, colors, and forms have resonance properties as well. You are a "resonant sound" struck by the source as it descended, like a surfer riding a wave, into a form.

Ideally, the combination in your body of its many resonances creates a majestic orchestra of harmonious beauty. Functionally, there is often something out of tune. You can learn to consciously repair your own energy system, with the resonance tools of *identification*, *repetition*, and *clearing*. You have been working with these tools of consciousness all along, only you may not have been aware of it.

Resonances are waves of consciousness that begin with a struck sound at a specific location and then vibrate out. With practice, we can learn to ride these waves of consciousness, just as if you were a surfer on Hawaii's North Shore. There, if you try to ride a wave too soon, you will fail to move very far. And if you try too late, you will get thrown around in the surf. But just right...and you have the thrill of uniting with great force and beauty, and moving smoothly, with great speed, to the wave's destination.

To understand how to ride a wave of consciousness, let's continue with our imagery of surfing and travel to

Hawaii's North Shore. As a novitiate surfer, you quickly discover there are many different opinions of how to most successfully navigate their huge, ten-foot high waves. So first you select one of these ways for study. Next, you learn to listen to and *identify* with what the instructor you have selected teaches you to do. Then you have to *repeat* this over and over, to master all the separate parts—when to catch the wave, how to stand up, how to shift your weight, and so on. As the learning process continues, you also have to learn to *clear* yourself of obstacles in your way— your fear of having the surfboard bang into you, the little mannerisms that creep into your style. You are taking the instruction provided you, working with it, and shaping it to your specific needs and personality. You are also identifying with the consciousness involved so closely that it becomes your own. Suddenly, it "clicks" into place and you are no longer external to the process but are inside, riding the wave in total oneness and harmony. Eventually, as the best surfers do, you know where the best waves are going to start and you position yourself accordingly, you and the wave moving together, as one. You have identified so closely with the sport that you are "one with its vibes" as a surfer might say; you are of the same resonance field.

When you ride waves of consciousness, you follow these same basic steps. Surfers of consciousness know it is possible to reach the goal of self-perfection by learning to resonate with someone else who has already achieved this. This is the basic reasoning behind discipleship to a spiritual master and, on a physical level, behind the Western principle of internship and apprenticeship. It is also possible, for those more oriented to jnana yoga, to learn to *resonate* with a specific consciousness, through these same principles of *identification*, *repetition*, and *clearing*.

Identification Tools

Identification is an empathic method of understanding which all healthy individuals do autonomically and many learn to do consciously. Autonomic refers to functions that go on inside our existence without our consciously willing it, such as our heart beating, our hair growing, and our assemblage point coinciding with that of our home environment. In energy work, we say people are empathetic when the capacity to identify with others and fully comprehend issues from perspectives different from their own. Empathic people have very mobile assemblage points.

Our human body system survives by resonant identification. We have discussed this with regard to our chakras and assemblage points, each of which resonates at a specific frequency. When we move away from a familiar resonance, we often initially feel uncomfortable, because the new frequency is not familiar to us.

Once you begin working with consciousness, you learn you have the choice to consciously identify with good or bad consciousness or resonance. You learn that the choices you make now cause resonant changes in your overall energy field. For example, you can choose to listen to discordant music, which through autonomic identification gradually throws your body's energy system off balance; or you can listen to soothing music, which autonomically contributes to a peaceful balancing of your system. The drumming in shamanic work and the singing of Benedictine monks are examples of positive sound; acid rock music is an example of discordant, unbalanced sound. Likewise, you can consciously choose to identify with angels or devils, spiritual masters or rogues, and each choice eventually leads you into very different dimensions, resonances, and consciousness.

Spiritual seekers make extensive use of identification to help elevate their consciousness or resonance. Shamans and energy workers use identification to shift their awareness or assemblage points into other dimensions of existence such as the awareness levels of medicinal plants or cosmic beings.

To assist in the process of identification, seekers will often concentrate on a physical artifact or symbol that resonates with the consciousness they are seeking. This item is being used as a tool to help one enter into that object's consciousness domain. In the health realms one might hold a stone or plant and identify with its resonance. In the spiritual realms one might focus on, hold, or wear the Zuni bear, the Christian cross, the Islamic hand of Fatima, the Buddhist and yogic Sri Yantra Mandala, the Mayan skull, the Chinese dragon, or the Jewish Star of David. You practiced the principles of identification in Exercises 1, 6, 11, 13, and 14, and will work with them again in Exercises 15, 17 and 18.

A very powerful tool in the identification realm is **visualization**. You can learn to see subtle consciousness with the inner eye. There are many meditation exercises that specifically teach seekers how to develop this awareness. They show you how to see or visualize an aspect of consciousness you wish to enter into and explore, identify with, and become.

Some humans are more comfortable visualizing consciousness in an Earth-related form and so consciousness obliges, appearing to seekers in a guise recognizable to their cultural conditioning. For example, the consciousness field of infinite love and compassion will appear to different people as a man (Christ), woman (Kwan Yin), god/goddess (Cupid, Venus, Lakshmi), saint (St. Theresa of Lisieux), holy being (Fatima), or even a site (Lourdes, Mt. Meru). We have practiced and will practice visualizing consciousness in Exercises 3, 4, 6, 12, 17, and 18.

Some people who are more comfortable working with abstract concepts or are very scientifically oriented often prefer to visualize consciousness as a form or pattern of energy such as a mandala or medicine wheel or the quality of peace or joy. Again consciousness obliges and appears in this form. We worked with a mandala in Exercises 7 and 8 and with visualizing peace as an aspect of many exercises in this book.

When a seeker of inner knowledge wishes to develop their ability to see the higher consciousness realms, spiritual master Sri Chinmoy recommends they cultivate the energies of **imagination**, **inspiration**, and **aspiration**. He advises a seeker to imagine, to seek the highest inspiration, and then aspire at all times to reach that goal. When you imagine some truly positive thing you wish to identify with and become, and begin working to achieve it, you set energies into motion that will change your life forever. Your *imagination*, your *inspiration* to be better than your are right now, and your *aspiration* to pursue your goal in spite of all obstacles helps you surf in the positive waves of the universe.

It helps to inspire yourself in practical ways. You can do this by keeping around you objects that both resonate with the consciousness of what you are seeking and help you move into this resonance. If you want peace in your life, you have the option of playing music that resonates with peace instead of with violence. You have the option of reading *The Celestine Prophecy* instead of Stephen King's latest horror novel. You have the option to watch television shows and videos that guide you toward peace instead of away from it. You have the option to associate with people who are inspiring instead of destructive. You have the option to attend gatherings whose objectives are peaceful instead of agitated. If those around you do not want to participate in these inspiring activities, you can use your ingenuity to protect yourself. This can range from using headphones to moving your desk to changing jobs or social groups. Choosing positive options helps you connect with the universe's positive waves of energy.

Identification tools operate in three separate stages: **concentration**, **meditation**, and **contemplation**. Concentration is the process of focusing on an object. In the realm of consciousness, concentration enables you to narrow your focus from the vast universe of options to one specific resonance, or object. Visually, it is like an archer who practices by first focusing on the circle of the target, then zeroes in on the dot in the middle, and then works to develop the skill to shoot the arrow into this point. Concentration is your arrow, which you direct at the bull's eye of your specific consciousness target. You practiced this in Exercises 1, 3, 7, and 8.

Meditation is an expansive process, a whole-field way of

experiencing an expanded consciousness. Once you learn to shoot the concentration-arrow and hit the bull's eye, a very interesting event occurs. You discover the bull's eye is actually a portal that opens into an entire new world of awareness. Alice experienced this when she stepped through the mirror into Wonderland. This world can possess a specific quality like peace or can be a specific place such as the mental or psychic plane of consciousness. You practiced this in Exercises 7 and 14.

Contemplation is concentrated focus from inside the whole-field experience of meditation. Once you have entered into this new world, and your inner sight adjusts, you begin to see there are specific energies and forms residing there. Eventually, you will wish to explore a specific aspect of this world. For example, inside the field of peace, one individual might wish to focus on how to relieve job stress while another might wish to focus on how to have a peaceful home life. Each would decide to focus on a different location inside the same broad consciousness field of peace, and contemplate what aspect of peace they need to encourage in their specific life situation. Contemplation was practiced in Exercises 9, 10, 12, 15.

Through the processes of concentration, meditation, and contemplation an individual makes progress toward fully exploring, identifying, becoming, and/or working with, whatever energy they have selected. All energy workers, healers, and spiritual individuals who are seeking to understand and work with consciousness make use of these tools. They may call them by other names, such as prayer and reflection, or shamanic travelling, but the underlying process is the same.

Some people experience semantic problems relating concentration, meditation, and contemplation to the Christian concepts of prayer and reflection. These are in essence the same processes of focus, expansion, and refocus. Prayer and concentration both involve focusing on an issue and seeking help from some aspect of consciousness. Reflection combines the processes of meditation and contemplation; it involves listening for the answer to your prayer and concentrating on how this answer will positively affect your particular issue.

The process of identification can be a conscious, positive tool for world development, but it can also be a negative one. If you do not believe that the inner worlds are a true reality that can affect you, you do not mind playing with the forces of darkness, for you consider them to be imaginary. We are experiencing the disastrous results of this near-sightedness throughout our Western culture right now. We are encouraging children and young adults to play video and computer games that glorify truly horrifying elements of violence and darkness, and are providing them with a wide variety of television shows and movies that make these dark forces seem powerful and empowering to the individual. Some people say it does not matter because these games and shows are only imaginary. They are not. They represent the energetic manifestation of very dark forces.

If we truly appreciated, understood, and valued the inter-relatedness of all life, these types of shows would not be possible. We are creating among our youth — the future of our nation — very dark and violent, interconnected group intent energy grids that are going to make it increasingly difficult for individuals to openly state they would prefer to work with the forces of light and not darkness. Any doubt about the imaginary nature of these forces is rapidly disappearing as we experience a growing range of violent outbreaks, directly based on popular entertainment stories. We need to introduce positive change that becomes so massive that, like the Hundredth Monkey, the American consciousness itself begins to change.

Exercise 15:
Identifying the Consciousness Inside Your Choices

Select some part of your life in which you are considering a change and are unsure of how to proceed. It could be deciding on a new job, lifestyle, or home. Focus on this situation and enter into it, using any of the principles from this book. Where will entering this world take you? Do you actually want to be there? Contemplate that world and see if it is one you want to grow into. See if you can discern the

various details inside the consciousness field of this world.
Will being there actually bring you full satisfaction? Or will
you soon tire and want something else? What do you feel
would bring you long-lasting happiness? What positive
changes in your choices could you make to move toward this
consciousness?

Repetition Tools

Repetition is another very powerful tool for affecting consciousness. Many traditions make use of repetition as a consciousness-linking and consciousness-reinforcing technique. Repetitive tools include chanting, moving meditations, and pranayama.

Chanting out loud or to yourself is a repetitive way to focus and establish your awareness within a specific plane of consciousness. You practiced chanting in Exercise 11.

Prayer beads such as malas, japa beads, and rosaries are often used by introspective traditions to help focus consciousness, to keep track of repetitive prayer rounds, and to ground consciousness in the physical act of handling the beads.

Let's look at some reasons why prayer beads are so effective. These necklaces are usually made of round beads which by the very nature of their physical shape exchange energy, back and forth, between the universal consciousness of the intent placed inside them, and your energy field. The complete strand of beads resonantly conducts and intensifies this energy by relaying it along the strand as you chant or pray, moving your fingers over each bead. A larger object is positioned at a central point, and called the guru bead, guide bead, or scapula. Like a physical guru or guide, this object protects the intent of the necklace's energy and removes unwanted energy. This can be via the tassel or, with a rosary, via a chain that leads to the Savior consciousness of the cross. You had the opportunity to do prayer rounds in Exercise 11.

In moving meditations, the balanced energies of meditation are brought into the gross physical world by larger repetitive body movement. This can be an important step in learning to maintain peace while in the activities of everyday life. We explored walking and running meditations in Exercise 14. Hatha yoga, qi gong, tai chi, and higher forms of the martial arts also work with these principles and often name their movements for the consciousness they are seeking to enter, such as the peacock, cobra, and warrior poses.

Pranayama, the science of breath control, is a gentle, subtle form of repetition to calm, center, and ground positive energy in the body system. You practiced a simple form of pranayama in Exercise 5. The following exercise is a more advanced form of pranayama.

Exercise 16:
Repetitive Breathing Exercise

In this exercise you are going to practice an alternate-nostril breathing exercise. When doing this, you can learn several things. First, you may discover that one or both of your nostrils is very clogged and you cannot breath easily through it. This reflects blockages in your subtle energy system. Second, you may not have been breathing deeply into your lungs and abdominal cavity, which implies that you energetically avoid breathing deeply of life in some way or another. Repeating this exercise for several days until you can sustain it without a break, or without cheating by taking an extra breath, will help you to balance and strengthen your energy flow. As you clear your breath, you begin to clear blockages in your consciousness as well.

Place the thumb and fourth finger of your right hand on either side of your nose. (You can use your left hand if you prefer.) Holding the left nostril closed with the fourth finger of your right hand, breathe in through the right nostril for two counts. Using thumb and fourth finger, keep both nostrils closed, and hold your breath for six counts. With your thumb closing your right nostril, release the finger on your left nostril and breathe out for four counts. Repeat this, only now breathe in the left nostril for two counts, holding for six counts, and breathe out the right nostril for four counts. Repeat this cycle for two minutes.

Clearing Tools

There is a perfect source of universal energy. That energy can be obstructed in various ways, such as through thoughts, feelings, and actions either internally generated or imposed upon us from the outside. If we can clear the energy obstructions, we can re-establish our connection to this source. Clearing is a very powerful tool in the resonance arsenal, and much is being done today in the fields of sound, light, and vibration to help people heal at all levels—physical, emotional, mental, and spiritual.

Some people find divining tools like the I Ching, tarot, pendulums, and crystal balls help them clear a path to their own higher self, to their inner guide, or to universal consciousness. These tools can help people find answers to specific questions that they cannot locate in other manners. You had the opportunity to work with a crystal ball in Exercise 8. Energy workers use these tools to quickly create a clear space and receive answers for their patients. When using these implements, one must remain detached from the question and the results because personal desire can affect the answers.

Clearing is a tool used in virtually all areas of energy work. Clearing the body's cells is being explored in medicine, from experimental treatments for cancer to removing the electromagnetic jamming of our body's energy grids caused by computers and other contemporary office equipment. Psychic healers seek to clear dysfunctional elements from the body. Chinese medicine works to clear the channels through which *chi*, or life energy, circulates.

Yogic master Sri Aurobindo believed that the human perfection yogis seek has to eventually include the cellular transformation of the human body, so that every cell of a soul's existence while on Earth is clear and permeated with the source's light.

Exercise 17:
Clearing by Visualization and Identification

Imagine you are on the top of a mountain, sitting in meditation. In front of you, also in meditation, is a golden child, emanating light and love. See the child calling you to come and play with them inside the light. Even if you feel some reservations, do your best to join the child. Enjoy the experience.

Now switch places. See yourself as the golden child and the child as the seeker. Call the child to come join you in the light. See what is keeping the child from doing so—what fear or reluctance—and inwardly clear that energetic obstruction by infusing it with light and love. While doing so, let the child know you love them and want nothing more than to be together with them in the light. See the child relax, release these obstructions, and gradually merge with you, in the light.

Switch places again and look at yourself facing this child who is now calling to you. Once again, join them, knowing now, experientially, just how much they truly want to be with you.

When you wish, return to the awareness of your own body, knowing the light of the child is now a part of you. Come out of meditation.

This child represents all the spiritual guides who seek to help us, and who use the tools of their own consciousness to elevate you into the higher energies.

Contacting and Working with Guides

A Guide Helps You Make Faster Progress

This book provides the reader with the basic information you need for the exploration of consciousness. It is enough to give you a feeling for the territory, and covers the various maps that are available to take you through it. You could, if you wish, explore this region on your own, but you will make much faster progress if you locate a qualified guide to assist you. For example, the very first European explorers of America took years to move from our East Coast to our West Coast: everything was new and unfamiliar and they had to face many dangers along with their exhilarating discoveries. Some of those who made it to the West Coast stayed and settled that territory while others came back, either carrying information or offering to serve as guides for those who wished to make this same journey.

Consciousness exploration—exploration of the inner worlds—is similar to this process, only it is housed inside yourself. You are your own final frontier, your own last unexplored world. Inner guides exist who can show you the way forward and help you reach your ultimate goal. They can provide you with the map of the territory you wish to explore. They are able to point out if you are taking the wrong route, if there are problems ahead that you could easily avoid, or if you must gear yourself up to fight.

Inner guides and maps are available at all levels, local to regional to universal, similar to outer guides. For example, you might use one guide to help you navigate the streets of Philadelphia and another to guide you through the vast territory between that city and San Francisco. Similarly, you might use one consciousness guide to learn the body's meridian system, another to show you how to read auras, while a third might be able to show you the entire territory from the physical world up to the source of life itself.

Guides exist everywhere in the universe, at all levels and in all dimensions. When you want to work with one, you need to determine the price they want to charge, the place they want to take you to, their level of authority and experience, and what authority figures they report to.

Initially you can accept or reject a person or force as

your guide. But once your journey is underway, it is often too late to go back. If you are on a liner in the middle of the Atlantic, you cannot suddenly change your travel plans from Africa to Asia. To change your travel plans, you have to travel through a series of connection, or assemblage, points and be considerably delayed in reaching your goal.

Here we are going to review the different kinds and levels of guides that exist in the world of consciousness. If you select your guide with care, and determine in advance what goal you wish to reach, you can make your trip much easier, safer, and faster.

What is a guide? What function does a guide serve? A guide is some being, energy, or consciousness with whom you can work to go somewhere. Webster's *New World Dictionary* defines a guide as "A person or thing that guides; specifically, through a region, building, etc. A person who directs, or serves as the model for, another in his conduct, career, etc."

Guides exist everywhere and we have always used them, whether we're aware of it or not. Whenever you ponder what to do or where to go next, you are seeking assistance from a guide. In this work, we are showing you the nature of consciousness guides and how, since the energy of the microcosm reflects the energy of the macrocosm, your knowledge of material reality will help you when you venture into the more subtle, and vaster, realms of consciousness.

There are guides on every level of every plane of every dimension of consciousness and for every route, whether this is toward the realms of light or darkness. The same qualities we see in our everyday world are also found in the subtle worlds and so consciousness guides come in many forms and at all levels of ability and knowledge. There are crooks and shysters, those who do their job but are not really interested, the deviously manipulative, the detached, and the passionately committed. In all these categories, guides can be incompetent, introductory level, experts, or geniuses.

The deeper, higher, and faster you want to travel, the more essential an expert, high-level guide becomes, and the harder they are to find. There are, for example, many beginner level music teachers but few who are truly master teachers. The master teachers are often the most strict, and they will often choose their students very carefully.

Once you subconsciously or consciously determine your intent, you will attract to yourself the appropriate guides for that region of exploration. You are resonating in their domain, and they respond. Whether you remain in their domain to study with them depends upon the bargain you strike together. Both sides must continue to meet each other's needs. Guides also have their duties to perform, and you should ascertain their intent before beginning your journey with them. There are ways to test the intent, purpose, and function of a consciousness guide, and they will be covered in this chapter.

The dominions of darkness and light operate in much the same way, since they are working with the same substance of consciousness. But the direction in which they travel is opposite to each other. Darkness works hard to make itself interesting by appealing to your desires. It often disguises itself as light and, if you do not look carefully, before you know it you have signed on for the trip.

The forces of light are not as pushy as is darkness and they are willing to leave the choice up to you whether you will travel toward the darkness or the light. They know that ultimately you must choose them, for the inherent drive of Earth's entire consciousness structure is to overcome all obstructions and return to the source of light. They also know your path must come from your own free will because, in order to succeed in your quest, you must choose to take the side of light, no matter how difficult that may be. So the forces of light will wait while you explore every form of darkness and debauchery, over lifetimes, if that is how you wish to proceed. When your soul is so tired of darkness that it cries out intensely for help, light energetically responds and brings you assistance in the form of light-beings from angels to spiritual masters.

This is one of the services darkness provides: it makes us so tired of itself that we learn to cling resolutely to the light.

In your search for a spiritual guide, the aid of an authentic spiritual master is an unparalleled boon. The role of the true spiritual master is to actively help human beings attain the light source. They are quite willing to battle to do so. There are many tales that describe how each master battles hostile forces to protect and reclaim disciples from the depths of darkness. The spiritual master willingly goes anywhere in the universe to rescue a devotee in need.

Whether you are living the life of a saint or are sick of your behavior, the role of the master is to show you how to overcome your weaknesses, subtle or gross, to attain the ultimate goal of life, which is oneness with the source.

Exercise 18:
Who or What Is Guiding You Now

Look at your everyday life. Look at how you behave and whether or not it serves your ultimate intent. Next look at the influences in your life: mass media, your friends and family, your job, your mother and father. Each are guides. What are they asking you to do? Perhaps you feel you are being forced to follow a certain path, or have no other option, but actually this is not so. Something in you has selected this particular path and these particular guides.

Now let's look at what happens if you consciously establish a new intent for your life, and look for an appropriate guide to help you on this journey. How will these changes affect the direction of your life and gradually every aspect of your life? Does what you see in the future please you or do you see trouble ahead? Envision choosing other routes and other guides and decide which goals you wish to attain.

Every journey begins with a single step. What will it take for you to make that one small initial step toward your goal? Determine to do this when you come out of meditation and begin.

Entering the Inner Worlds — A Westerner's First Steps

Each culture contributes something unique to our global consciousness. The Far East has learned to see existence as a continuum of consciousness, top to bottom. It sees life forms existing at every level, each of whom has its own responsibilities and often interacts with human beings. The Judeo-Christian West separates this continuum into three separate domains: Heaven, Earth, and Hell. It says that since the domain of humans is Earth, we should focus our attention on perfecting our world and leave the others to work in theirs.

These intents are so vastly different in perspective that they have fostered belief systems that are also vastly different from each other. Each is equally valid but each has focused on only part of the issue at hand: how consciousness works in totality, and specifically for Earth. Together, the two approaches provide a much more complete picture of how consciousness works and, when we include the knowledge of other cultures, such as the Islamic and the indigenous traditions of our world, our picture becomes even more complete. Today, our world is also learning from cultures existing in other dimensions of the universe—cultures that are establishing contact with us in many different ways from channeling to visions to subtle and gross physical communication.

Every culture has its strengths and its weaknesses. Because the Far East sees the broad view of consciousness, it is often overwhelmed by humanity's smallness in the vast universe. The East's viewpoint tends to fatalism and inaction, a belief in predestination, and a belief that the gross physical plane is limited and constricts us energetically.

Because the West wished to separate consciousness into three separate domains, and focus on perfecting the one we inhabit, it has gradually become blind to the activities of the other two regions. If we caught a glimpse of another region, we tried to ignore or reject it and soon we grew to fear these worlds because of our lack of understanding. From that fear grew many constraints on venturing into the other regions of consciousness, first warning, then forbidding, and then punishing anyone who ventured into those territories.

Today, cultures are learning from and sharing with each other. Knowledge helps dissipate fear. The West is showing the East not to fear the physical, and the standard of living of the Eastern worlds is markedly improving. The East, and our own indigenous cultures, are showing the mainstream West not to fear the inner worlds.

As the Western Judeo-Christian world begins to explore the vast realms of consciousness, we have two major issues that we need to overcome. These are a sense of guilt and a lack of discrimination. Both these issues come specifically from our attempts to isolate the Earth experience and focus on its gross physical issues.

Guilt is an attempt to impose restrictions on an individual contrary to their own personal inclinations, good or bad. It is often supported by physical punishment, imprisonment, or death. For many centuries, Western Judeo-Christian culture attempted to inculcate a sense of guilt, supported by the moral and legal clout of church and state, to prevent individuals from exploring domains other than that of the gross physical. The only outlet we had to explore these worlds was through science "fiction," a form distinctly Western in derivation. The same issues and forces we find in science fiction, other cultures find in their mainstream cultural, philosophical, and spiritual works: interaction with cosmic forces, communication with beings from other dimensions, travel through space and time, and so on.

Western mainstream culture created in its people a real fear of exploring anything subtle that was not in keeping with official doctrine. We did so by burning explorers as witches and heretics, throwing them into prisons or locking them in mental asylums and declaring them insane. Insane asylums are another invention of the West.

But like all darkness this type of persecution, based in fear, is coming to an end. It has played itself out; it has explored every control device possible and is still not able to stop our inherent human drive to expand our knowledge. Our culture is now working with a different approach: education. Through education, we are learning proper discrimination. We are learning, but it is a slow process that must filter through our culture, just like washing food with the Hundredth Monkey. One function of this book is to help hasten the learning curve that creates a cultural shift in awareness of consciousness.

Because, historically, mainstream Western society has not focused awareness on the inner worlds, we are now experiencing the problems that come with learning about something unfamiliar. During the exploratory period of the 1960s–1990s, a mere thirty years, the West has made tremendous progress, but we still have a lot to learn.

We are slowly learning not to accept the subtle energetic

forces that come our way at face value without examining their true intent or purpose. For example, right now we are entertained by video games, art and books, videos, TV, and movies that are all too often teaching our youth to glorify darkness. With a new focus of understanding we could glorify light just as well as we do darkness. We are learning that if we do not connect freedom with conscious awareness we are all too often letting our children play with the subtle aggressive energies of hatred, fear, and black magic. Instead of, through education and entertainment, showing our youth how to identify with an elevated consciousness, we are teaching our youth to identify with destructive guides—murderers who take the law into their own hands or kill for sport.

We are learning, slowly, to distinguish true positive inner guidance from false glamour. Tales abound of what happens when we choose not to see what happens in the subtle world of consciousness. Sometimes we find authentic inner guides but we also follow disastrous fakes such as Jim Jones and Charles Manson and the false spiritual masters whose escapades have been strewn across our papers these last few decades.

Choosing an Inner Guide

There will always be a need for guides, whether it is the need of youngsters learning about how life should or could function or adults seeking to become expert in some field of knowledge.

Americans always want freedom. But true freedom comes as a result of strength and knowledge. Right now many are accepting any force that offers to guide them into the inner worlds at face value, because they don't know how to discriminate. Some simple, matter-based ways for you to know if the guide you choose is genuine are to check the guide's credentials, clearly examine the experiences and lives of the members of your guide's group, notice how the guide expresses anger and frustration, examine what the guide claims is their source, see if that source clearly resonates the truth, and learn to see for yourself.

Seeking Help

When we Westerners enter the inner realms of consciousness knowledge for the first time, to seek help and guidance, often it's like turning on a radio and hearing all frequencies at once. You have to make a choice as to which frequency you want to focus on. At first, you may experience a collective static or white noise, which can feel like a boring or frustrating state of nothingness. You may be overwhelmed by sensations, flooded by sights, sounds, feelings, colors, or music that threaten to overwhelm your internal balance. In either case, you need to stop, stand still, and tune in to the energy. To do so, you use the tools of consciousness we have been working with throughout this book, including the most basic tools of discrimination: concentration, meditation, and contemplation.

If you already have a bona fide guide, a master, or a definite path or philosophy, or have had a strong commitment to a guide or master in a past life, your soul has already established a path to some of the higher levels of the inner worlds. Upon initially entering the inner worlds, you may experience a re-contact with some part of that world, which may be far different from the way in which you experience your present existence. For example, you may be Christian yet find you have profound love for the Buddha. This affection does not mean you need to change your current path if you don't wish to, but the knowledge you previously acquired has the potential to integrate and enrich your present life.

When a Guide Approaches You:

Some guides, though benign in nature and willing to help, don't usually initiate contact. They may make contact through the information you seek. For example, through seeking information on the Universe's Consciousness Library, known by yogis as the Akashic Records, you may enter into contact with guides of this group.

Some guides may choose to communicate with you through the cultural orientation with which you are most familiar. Peace, love, and wisdom, for example, are universal consciousnesses but, as we have discussed before, they will often appear in different guises depending upon one's culture, need, and level of awareness.

Sometimes, when you're not listening and the inner worlds need to communicate with you, guides will inwardly grab your attention, so to speak, to make you aware of their presence. Channeling, visions, apparitions, voices, and appearances are forms of this type of contact.

There are also mischievous and hostile guides who may contact you to fulfill their function, which is to delay or distract you from increased awareness. They can take various shapes as an enticement to win you over to their side. They may offer you powers and promise to fulfill your desires. Then, when they tire of the game, they take the powers away or watch the powers achieve their goal, which is to destroy you. Many magicians and black occultists have come to power and fame and eventually mysteriously died in this way. The guides of darkness can take control of your existence only if you succumb to their enticements, which is why personal will power and strength of character are so prized by all cultures. Christ's temptation in the desert, when the Devil appeared and offered up the world if the Christ would only follow him, is the supreme example in the West of the use of personal will power and purity of character to reject the entice-ments of darkness.

In the beginning of your studies, you may wonder how you can know if a guide is beneficent or bad. Each soci-ety has developed ways to test, but all focus on the power of intent and personal will power as the best natural pro-tective forces of the universe. Once you have your own bona fide guides, they become your protective forces, too. There are a number of ways to determine the intent of the guides. Chant the name of God from your faith over and over; darkness cannot stand the presence of light and will withdraw or even explode into nothingness. If you find you cannot chant God's name in the beings' presence, then beware! Declare your intent to move forward only into light and call for help from all the beneficent forces of the universe. Use your senses. If there is an acrid odor associated with the beings, beware. If they promise you power, fame, and fortune, instead of personal self-perfection, stay clear.

However, if you simply feel uneasy, ask them why they want to help you, and carefully assess their explanation. Feeling uneasy can be a warning, can reflect a human unwillingness to change, or can come from the indecisive confusion that naturally occurs when you stand in the mid-dle of a crossroads and need to decide which way to go next.

Categories of Guides

There are three general categories of guides: human guides, nature and cosmic entities related to the earth plane of consciousness, and entities and beings from other dimensions.

Human Guides

Human guides are those beings who are maturing through the experience of life on Earth. They have mastered some element of this process and can help others travel their route as well. We utilize human guides whenever we want to learn something, whether it is crocheting a baby sweater, constructing an office building, learning to deal with stress, or achieving the goal of self-perfection.

In all subjects, we proceed by grade level. Sometimes we keep the same human teacher and sometimes we switch. It is very rare to stay with one guide throughout this process of growth, although there are master teachers who can act as guides throughout a student's life.

There are human guides who are very advanced beings and who have consciously chosen to remain in the Earth consciousness to serve as a link or bridge connecting other humans to the inner realms of consciousness. Usually, when human life is over, we take rest before assuming another form and continuing our task. But some great souls wish to continue their teaching or service function by remaining just beyond the physical realm, in interim planes, to serve as guides for those seeking spiritual knowledge. We find tales of these great souls scattered throughout all traditions. They include the bodhisattvas of the Buddhist traditions; some saints; and some yogis such as the legendary Babaji who has for centuries existed in the Himalayas, appearing in subtle form to seekers in need around the world.

The great spiritual masters of Earth's history comprise another category of human guide. Specifically, they help to bring humanity to the light. The great spiritual masters' purpose is addressing imbalances between light and dark, protecting the meek and weak, and ushering in a new age of awareness. Yogis call these rare individuals avatars. They include Christ, Buddha, Krishna, and others. It is the rarest and most profound blessing for a soul to be in the presence of these individuals while they are on Earth. You will make remarkable progress if you ever have this blessing.

Once the great masters leave their physical body, they continue serving God and Earth from the inner worlds. Each avatar has their own distinct inner realm in which they reside, called a loka by yogis and heaven by Christians. Profound devotees will often rest in their master's loka or heaven between incarnations. Each master's inner world is a distinct realm. This is why some disciples of some masters state with absolute conviction that only they are "saved." They don't sense any one from other faiths in their particular heaven. While what they see is true, it is not the whole truth. Their heaven is for their faith, but other faiths have their heavens, too.

The inner worlds of the great masters increase in size over time. A whole range of existences, from many dimensions, assist this world in caring for its devotees on Earth. If you are a part of a great master's world, beings from their realm will come to assist you if you need help. All will identify the master they serve.

Sometimes souls come to Earth to serve their master's world in some specific way. The consciousness they create on Earth remains after they leave. Yet this soul may continue incarnating for their own further growth. Thus it is that some individuals, when looking into their past lives, see they have been a great yogi or a saint still revered by millions of people, yet they know they are still a long way from the ultimate human goal of self-perfection.

Nature and Cosmic Entities Related to Earth

Nature and cosmic entities related to Earth have been placed in charge of specific domains of consciousness by the Supreme. These entities have a direct relationship to our planet and our planet's existence. These beings can be good, mischievous, or bad. They communicate, associate, teach, and help you within the framework of their influence, according to your level of development. Like humans, these beings occupy many different levels of many different disciplines. They range from fairies and wood sprites to cosmic gods and goddesses to angels. They can manifest as qualities like wisdom and love or as beings like Athena or Venus.

These beings serve the Supreme in some task-specific manner. Angels, for example, have the special job of caring for and protecting humans, and carrying messages to humans from God. Nature entities might be responsible for a specific site, such as a forest glen; an aspect of a realm, such as a specific animal, herb, or type of stone; or an entire "division" such as all crystals or all animals. Shamans and medicine men and women often work with guides from this category to find and retrieve healing information and capacities. Cosmic entities can also serve a specific consciousness such as love; a craft, such as art; or an occupation, such as a policeman. Many cultures have gods and goddesses who are the patron protective force for specific occupations, functions, or geographical areas.

There are also collective entities—beings who work together to sustain life. These include entities who maintain the grids of energy that circle our Earth; and the gandharvas—cosmic musicians who sit in eternal concert, playing celestial music and inspiring human musicians.

Cosmic and nature guides have specific realms of influence. Once they accept you, they will show you their terrain, at first providing a surface tour, and gradually going into greater detail. However, they have no particular interest in helping humans attain the ultimate goal of God-realization. In fact, to retain their supremacy, some of them, such as the cosmic gods and guardians, often attempt to delay a seeker from moving past them to the source. So eventually, after struggling to enter their world, you may have to struggle again to leave it. This is the difference between working with a cosmic force, who is responsible for a specific territory, and a human spiritual master, whose God-ordained responsibility is to help you consciously return to the source.

Entities and Beings from Other Dimensions

There are many, many dimensions and universes inside creation. Earth occupies only one of these. Entities in other worlds have been busy mastering their dimensions, just as we have been mastering ours, and some are much farther along than we are. Entities from these worlds—good and bad—have been coming to Earth to explore and affect our development for a long, long time. Spiritual masters, visionaries, and occultists throughout the ages have been aware of these entities and they have talked and written about them. You will find references to these interactions, often disguised, in spiritual, esoteric, and occult literature and in many pictographs, mandalas, and visionary and symbolic paintings.

There are many, many reasons why these entities and beings come to Earth. These entities have their own objectives which may or may not be compatible with ours. Some want to help us become more aware of the true nature of who we are as spiritual beings. Some come from advanced beneficent races who want to help us enter the galactic community in a peaceful, positive fashion. Some come with advanced technology and information, to help us move forward quickly in some manner. Some seek to elevate the genetic capacity of our species, through biological union. Some come from curiosity, scientific study, adventure or trade. Some have dark and hostile intents.

These visitors have often provided evidence of their presence that we are just beginning to acknowledge and explore. These include: crop circles, giant earth mounds, ancient Mayan and Aztec galactic time markings on stone monuments, ancient Egyptian material, depictions of space ships and extra-terrestrials in many ancient to modern drawings, and UFO sightings and interactions around the world (some authentic and some not).

Today, as Earth enters a critical period in our evolutionary growth, contact with these beings is occurring in many different ways. It is reaching such proportions that we are switching over from denial to scientific exploration. This is similar to the change in awareness that has occurred every time our world has expanded its parameters of knowledge. It is the Hundredth Monkey Principle yet again.

Contact can be for good or bad purposes, depending on the type of being. It is for your personal highest good if communication is conscious, via one of the higher levels of the planes of which humans are formed—the soul, heart, mind, and vital. Contact can also occur through channeled information, which involves a being overriding a human's conscious awareness with its own. There is subtle physical or gross physical materialization of a being from another dimension into ours. And, finally, there is transportation of a human to the being's own realms, for instruction, on various consciousness levels from the soul to the physical planes.

Special Cases

Some people on Earth have incarnated here from other dimensions. Especially from those dimensions that have a close connection to Earth. These include the fairy, angel, and cosmic god realms and also other worlds such as the Pleiades and Sirius. We are becoming more aware of this now, as our capacity to see into consciousness increases.

In general, beings from other dimensions and worlds who choose to incarnate on Earth do so because they love Earth and want to experience our particular type of world.

They may have been helping us for eons from the subtle realms, and decide they want to descend into physical form to experience precisely the contours and issues of our life form. They want to assist us in a very direct way, in the gross physical body. Because of the amnesia that accompanies human birth, they may not be aware of who they are and where they come from. But at a certain time in their life, perhaps when they are under severe stress and are, with all their soul's strength, calling for help, beings and guides from their own worlds may contact them. These beings are related to their own integral development and should be listened to, along with listening to the advice of a human spiritual master, who can help the person adapt to the highest goals of this world.

Another rare situation is found in a number of esoteric groups that are seeking to overcome the amnesia that accompanies human birth. Ordinarily, a very high being or soul must be born and achieve its goal from scratch. All souls risk failure because to date the process of birth on Earth, which drops spirit into gross matter, can make even the highest soul forget its mission. There are many stories in yogic history of individuals leading very ordinary lives, then suddenly waking up and remembering that they had originally incarnated to fulfill a very important God-requested task. Tibetan Buddhism works with this issue, and has found ways to ascertain where the souls of their most advanced priests and lamas have reincarnated. They will physically send older lamas with items from the child's past, to reawaken and assist them to return to their spiritual path.

The Melchizedek orders work on occasion with paired contracts between souls to enable a very high mission to take place; they call this the "walk in." This occurs only in very special circumstances, for instance when a very high spiritual entity, or human, needs to incarnate at a very specific time and place to accomplish a very important task, and the order does not wish to risk failure from loss of the soul via birth amnesia. In this pre-birth arrangement, two souls or beings make a soul's contract with each other, one serving as host to prepare the body, and the other promising to replace the first at the appropriate time. This second individual will often serve as a guide, assisting the host as they are growing up, although because of birth amnesia the host may not be aware of who is helping them. When the time comes for the switch to take place, the two may exchange places, or share the body during an adaptive period. Then, the work of the first soul now completed, it leaves and returns to the soul's world, and the new soul takes up residence, working from the start in full power and awareness of its purpose. There are some significant path breakers at work today who openly acknowledge this exchange has taken place. They include

Anna Hayes (whose Melchizedek name is Aneayhea Kananda Melchizedek) and Drunvalo Melchizedek.

Selecting Your Guide

When deciding whom to work with as guides, stay alert. Find out precisely where the guides comes from, and their objective in working with you. We are not alone in wanting to expand our knowledge of creation. All life forms are interested in doing so. But just because a life form has knowledge different from our own, it does not make them superior to us, and they do not necessarily mean us well even if they assure us this is so. We should not blindly accept guides without ascertaining who they are and what they want to accomplish.

If you come into contact with entities from other dimensions, you need to be careful and wise in ascertaining the purpose and intent of the being you encounter. Do not naively accept help from subtle beings without understanding, as much as possible, the true nature of the entity. You always need to be careful about accepting a ride from a stranger! You should look at this initial contact like an ordinary business exchange, where nothing is free — everything has a price. Whatever route you choose to take, whatever offer a potential guide makes, carefully consider the hidden costs. What is the price, the nature, and the quality of the product being offered? What is the function and goal of the guide and its product?

A careful checking out is necessary when such contact is initiated. This is especially true with the channeling of entities that is becoming so popular nowadays. There is a difference between channeling and communicating with entities. Channeling means you serve as a conduit for information. Communicating means you maintain your individual will and can choose what you wish to do with the information you receive. There is a very vast difference between learning to communicate with these existences and surrendering your free will to them by letting them take over your existence. While some channeling serves a purpose, of imparting information, it is always better for you to do the hard work and acquire the ability to consciously see into and work with the material being offered.

Some people seek to help Earth by permitting highly evolved entities from our own or other dimensions to use their body and voice to relay advanced technical information to Earth. In this case channeling is serving a technical function, for the transfer of information, but it is not serving the function of transforming our own personal existence for self-knowledge. The spiritual masters teach that for us to truly serve in a wise and integral manner, we need to develop our infinite potentials and knowledge for ourselves.

You Are Your Own Best Guide
The highest and most significant human course of action,

advocated by the greatest spiritual figures throughout Earth history, is for you to find a true master of spirit and consciousness, living or deceased, from Earth or one of its universe's higher dimensions, and learn for yourself the greatest art and science of all: self-awareness. A true master will help you make inner progress far beyond anything you have dreamed of. Once you are working with a spiritual master, you will begin encountering guides who will help you according to your personal necessity within the master's safe environment. And whatever further exploration you undertake on your own will have the benefit of your spiritual master's guidance and protection.

No matter who you select as your guides, you should always keep your right to self-control and maintain your personal free will to obey or not obey your guides' requests, to follow or not follow their teachings. The greatest guides of consciousness teach that free will is the central principle of existence on Earth. These masters often seem difficult and demanding, but they are actually requiring that, at every moment, you make the choice for yourself whether to move farther into the light, or whether to stop for a time, or whether to turn around on your trip to your own source-goal. They know that to succeed, in this greatest of all cosmic explorations, the choice must always be up to you.

Resource Guide

Abraham, Ralph. *Chaos, Gaia, Eros*. San Francisco: Harper Collins, 1994.

Andrews, Shirley. *Atlantis: Insights from a Lost Civilization*. Minnesota: Llewellyn Publications, 1997.

Arguelles, Jose & Miriam. *Mandala*. Boston: Shambhala, 1995.

Arguelles, Jose. *The Mayan Factor: Path Beyond Technology*. New Mexico: Bear & Co., 1996.

Aurobindo, Sri. *The Life Divine*. Wisconsin: Lotus Light Publications, 1990.

Bowman, Catherine. *Crystal Awareness*. Minnesota: Llewellyn Publications, 1992.

Braden, Gregg. *Awakening to Zero Point: The Collective Initiation*. Washington: LL Productions, 1994.

Briggs, John & Peat, F. David. *Turbulent Mirror: An Illustrated Guide to Chaos Theory and the Science of Wholeness*. New York: Harper & Row, 1990.

Chinmoy, Sri. *Beyond Within: A Philosophy for the Inner Life*. New York: Agni Press, 1988.

Chinmoy, Sri. Can be contacted c/o AUM Publications, 150-30 86th Ave., Jamaica, NY 11432. (718) 523-1423.

Chinmoy, Sri. *My Flute*. New York: Agni Press, 1975.

Chinmoy, Sri. *The Wings of Joy*. New York: Fireside Books, Simon & Schuster, 1997.

Chinmoy, Sri. *Yoga and the Spiritual Life*. New York: Agni Press, 1974.

Crystal Life Technology, Inc. 161-48 Normal Rd., Jamaica, NY 11432. Telephone: 1-800-871-9985. Web site: www.crystal-life.com

Frawley, Dr. David. *Tantric Yoga and the Wisdom Goddesses: Spiritual Secrets of Ayurveda*. Delhi: Motilal Banarsidass Publishers, 1997.

Fuentes, Starr. Casa Alma Retreat Center, Rt. 2 Box 3403, Navasota, TX 77868. (408) 894-3447. Web site: www.starrfu.com

Galde, Phyllis. *Crystal Healing: The Next Step*. Minnesota: Llewellyn Publications, 1993.

Gardner, Joy. *Color and Crystals: A Journey Through the Chakras*. California: The Crossing Press. 1996.

Gerber, Richard, M.D. *Vibrational Medicine*. New Mexico: Bear & Company, 1954.

Gleick, James. *Chaos: Making a New Science*. New York: Penguin Books, 1987.

Gold, Peter. *Navajo & Tibetan Sacred Wisdom: The Circle of the Spirit*. Vermont: Inner Traditions, 1994.

Haich, Elisabeth. *Initiation*. California: Seed Center, 1974.

Halevi, Z'ev ben Shimon. *Kabbalah: Tradition of Hidden Knowledge*. England: Thames & Hudson, 1992.

Hay, Louis L. *You Can Heal Your Life*. California: Hay House, Inc., 1987.

Hayes, Anna. Voyagers International. 1751 Tangelo Dr., Sarasota, FL 34239. (212) 462-9257. Web site: www.annahayes.com

Hayes, Anna. *Voyagers: The Secrets of Amenti, Vol. II*. North Carolina: Granite Publishing, 1999.

Hayes, Anna. *Voyagers: The Sleeping Abductees, Vol. I*. North Carolina: Granite Publishing, 1999.

Johari, Harish. *Chakras: Energy Centers of Transformation*. Vermont: Destiny Books, 1987.

Jung, C.G. *Mandala Symbolism*. New Jersey: Princeton University Press, 1972.

Khanna, Madhu. *Yantra: The Tantric Symbol of Cosmic Unity*. Great Britain: Thames & Hudson, 1994.

Lawlor, Robert. *Sacred Geometry*. England: Thames & Hudson, 1994.

Light Years Ahead Productions. *Light Years Ahead: the Illustrated Guide to Full Spectrum and Colored Light in Mindbody Healing*. California: Celestial Arts, 1996.

MacIagan, David. *Creation Myths: Man's Introduction to the World*. England: Thames & Hudson, 1992.

MacKenzie, Linda. *Inner Insights: The Book of Charts*. California: Creative Health & Spirit, 1996.

Meadows, Kenneth. *Earth Medicine: A Shamanic Path to Self Mastery*. England: Element Books Ltd., 1989.

Melchizedek, Drunvalo. *The Ancient Secret of the Flower of Life, Vol. 1*. Arizona: Light Technology Publishing, 1998.

Raleigh, A.S. *Occult Geometry*. California: DeVorss & Company, 1932.

Rivera A., Adalberto. *The Mysteries of Chichen Itza*. Rome: Universal Image Enterprise, Inc., 1995.

Schneider, Michael S. A *Beginner's Guide to Constructing the Universe*. Harper Perennial, 1995.

Sharamon, Shalila and Baginski, Bodo J. *The Chakra-Handbook*. Wisconsin: Lotus Light Publications, 1991.

Sitchin, Zecharia. *The 12th Planet*. New York: Avon Books, 1978.

Weiss, Brian, M.D. *Many Lives, Many Masters*. New York: Fireside Books, Simon & Schuster, 1988.

Yogananda, Paramahansa. *Autobiography of a Yogi*. California: Self-Realization Fellowship, 1979.

Index

Books by The Crossing Press

All Women Are Psychics
By Diane Stein

Women's intuition is no myth; women really are psychic. But your inborn psychic sense was probably suppressed when you were very young. This inspiring book will help you rediscover and reclaim your dormant psychic aptitude.

$16.95 • Paper • ISBN 0-89594-979-2

Chakras and Their Archetypes: Uniting Energy Awareness and Spiritual Growth
By Ambika Wauters

Linking classic archetypes to the seven chakras in the human energy system can reveal unconscious ways of behaving. Wauters helps us understand where our energy is blocked, which attitudes or emotional issues are responsible, and how to then transcend our limitations.

$16.95 • Paper • ISBN 0-89594-891-5

Channeling for Everyone: A Safe Step-by-Step Guide to Developing Your Intuition and Psychic Awareness
By Tony Neate

This is a clear, concise guide to developing our subtler levels of consciousness. It provides us with safe, step-by-step exercises to prepare for and begin to practice channeling, allowing wider states of consciousness to become part of our everyday lives.

$12.95 • Paper • ISBN 0-89594-922-9

Essential Reiki: A Complete Guide to an Ancient Healing Art
By Diane Stein

This bestseller includes the history of Reiki, hand positions, giving treatments, and the initiations. While no book can replace directly received attunements, Essential Reiki provides everything else that the practitioner and teacher of this system needs, including all three degrees of Reiki, most of it in print for the first time.

$18.95 • Paper • ISBN 0-89594-736-6

BOOKS BY THE CROSSING PRESS

A New Approach to the Alexander Technique: Moving Toward a More Balanced Expression of the Whole Self

By Glen Park

The Alexander Technique has long been recognized throughout the world as a powerful method for unlearning unconscious, habitual behavior, alleviating physical and mental stress, and encouraging personal growth and transformation. This book offers fascinating insights into how we function, with a methodology for allowing change to happen.

$18.95 • Paper • ISBN 0-89594-918-0

Peace Within the Stillness: Relaxation & Meditation for True Happiness

By Eddie and Debbie Shapiro

Meditation teachers Eddie and Debbie Shapiro teach a simple, ancient practice which will enable you to release even deeper levels of inner stress and tension. Once you truly relax, you will enter the quiet mind and experience the profound, joyful, and healing energy of meditation.

$14.95 • Paper • ISBN 0-89594-926-1

Shaman in a 9 to 5 World

By Patricia Telesco

A complete guide to maintaining a powerful connection with nature, even when sacred groves and wild rivers are far away. Patricia Telesco adapts an array of ancient shamanic traditions to city life, including fasting, drumming, praying, creating sacred spaces, interpreting omens, and divination.

$14.95 • Paper • ISBN 0-89594-982-2

To receive a current catalog from The Crossing Press
please call toll-free, 800-777-1048.
Visit our Web site: **www.crossingpress.com**